CONTENTS

FOREWORD 3
THANKS 5
CASE FOR THE BOOK 6
INTRODUCTION 8
PART I, NETWORK – MARKETING 12
Beginnings 12
Orientation, how does it work and why? 14
Motivations 22
Conclusions 23
Lies and false beliefs. 26
PART II, MLM NETWORK BUILDER GUIDANCE SYSTEM 35
Setting the targets (goals) 37
The list of names 45
The invitation 55
Presenting the Opportunity 1:1 (first meeting) 64
The second meeting (Answering objections and finalizing the first discussion) 71
Professional start (business initiation) 86
Tools and events 104
PART III, TOOLS FOR MAKING THE DREAMS COME TRUE 107
Time Management 107

Discipline in six steps   114
Attitude   119
Small non verbal communication guide   123
Perseverance   135
In life everything happens for a reson! Three magic
words: thoughts become things   142
CLOSURE   145

FOREWORD

Today I have the honor to write the foreword for this book, **SECRETS OF AN EXPONENTIAL BUSINESS**, signed by my good friend Dragoș Bălan. What this book represents is the first step that one of us, a normal Romanian person with worries and fears, desires and dreams, takes in order to give something from his experience to those who want to make something out of the patterns of a rigid society, for a better life.

These words are addressed to all those who want more. The author is above all a Prometheus of everyday life. The society forced each cell of his body to give its best in order to be able to live and sometimes to survive for his goal ... that is to live outside bars or above bars.

These words are for those who do not accept explicitly or indirectly authoritarianism as a way of life or organization. It is a writing for those for whom freedom is not just a right. It is a book for those for whom freedom is an obligation. Dragoș Bălan writes here the recipe for each of us to be able to tackle a journey of personal development by creating an intelligent social network.

What does that mean? It means to give in the end something from yourself to every man you meet and towards whom you feel the need to make an extra step for creating a relationship. A relationship which, multiplied, can lead to both professional fulfillment and the most important accomplishment, the personal one. Network marketing, also known generally as MLM is actually concentrated life. It's actually a good set of principles that make you understand quicker how this society works. Someone said that we born alone and we die alone. I say that neither we born alone because there are those who help us come into the world, nor we die alone because there are the ones who lead us in the way to the other side ... and above all we do not live alone ever.

To live in the society and in the social network which we belong, the right thing is what Dragoş Bălan's book teaches us, who after major successes in network marketing manages to point out a fundamental thing, namely that the art of leadership is based not only on actions and matrixes, but fundamentally on people; people that the author loves and learns to love every day, sending us this continuing effort through each page. Read this book to the last page. Out of respect for the author who lives each day following the principles related here - out of respect for the respect that he has as an edifice for all people.

Dr. Codrin Scutaru

THANKS

THANKS

Writing a book of any kind it may be seems to be an individual project, but in fact many people have contributed to the issue of this material, due to all those experiences that I had with them.

First I want to thank my life partner, Nicoleta for the unconditional trust she has in me. I would also like to thank my parents, Angela and Victor Bălan, for their love and support throughout my whole life;
I appreciate and I am proud that such quality people have been or are beside me, people who have helped me to make progress in building a network and I thank everyone who guided me.
And last but not least many thanks to all authors, speakers, mentors and leaders who have inspired me and showed me a way that through this work, I try myself to show to others.

CASE FOR THE BOOK

"The sign of true richness stands in what a person can give forward"- T. Harv Eker

I can still remember how I first read by myself a story, a fairytale and I dreamed then that anything is possible. Later in my teeanage days I read almost everything I could lay hands on, from philosophy to personal development and motivational books. Then, after college, there was a break, the books were replaced with other activities, since I had read enough before, I needed life experience and practical situations then. But now I know that most of the things I possess I could have not access only through my own experience. Luckily I could read, learn and inspire from other people's thoughts and actions. I am not a big fan of classical education system, but I appreciate very much the books. Later, that's why I started reading again, looking in "training the mind" for the kerosene for a journey through life towards success with less turbulences. I'm still on the road but I'm glad that I already know now that "success is a journey and not a destination."

I realized that all the experience in a field, whatever this may be, is pretty much nothing unless it is shared. I firmly believe that sharing everything I know and helping others is the best way of helping me. Regarding all that you will read here, I certaintly don't claim that I invented hot water, all that is written here is inspired by other materials, written or audio, from ideas found on the internet (I'm glad Internet potential is unlimited) and from Conferences held by inspirational speakers and network-marketing industry leaders across the planet. I wanted to offer a simple and understandable summary to all those who seek to know what are the tools for an opportunity that may become a dream business for everyone.
I wrote this book to make you understand what building a network means, why and how to do it. It will show you the basic steps for starting such a business. It was written for those who are now starting and also for those who are considering to re-start this activity. I wrote this work hoping that it will reach those who need it as much as I needed this information a few years ago when I started as an independent distributor in the network-marketing industry.

And most of all I wish that this book will help you discover new skills that you never knew you had and to develop new habits, so that you successfully use the power of network, both in business and in personal life!

INTRODUCTION

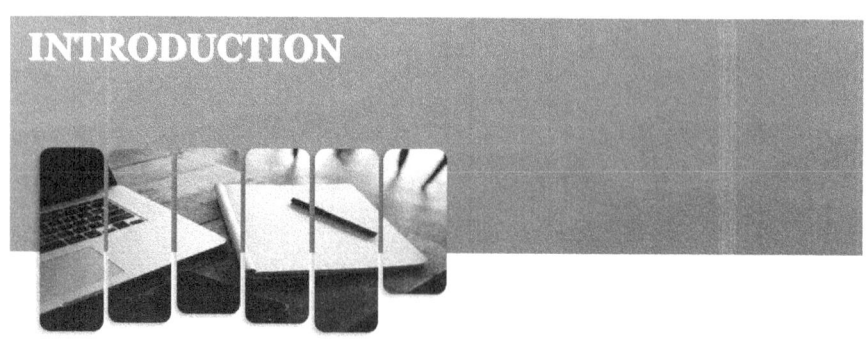

A GREAT OPPORTUNITY OF THE PRESENT

First I want to congratulate you because you are among those looking for an opportunity. Having your own business is a more or less spoken dream to most of the people. But only those seeking for opportunities and then act will succeed.

This way I let you know that there is a way for an ordinary person to start a business and run yearly products and services from thousands to millions of dollars. It is a great business that leverages the extraordinary power of personal recommendation, social network and Internet.

This way I let you know that there is a way for an ordinary person to start a business and run yearly products and services from thousands to millions of dollars. It is a great business that leverages the extraordinary power of personal recommendation, social network and Internet. For example, nowadays, thanks to the Internet, you can get in contact with an infinite number of potential customers or partners and not just with those living near you. Think of the hundreds of thousands or even millions of people you can contact through social networks. Using Skype made disappearing phone costs and videoconferences are making practically possible to gather in a "large room" people from all over the world.

Network marketing is now an opportunity for anyone who wants to start their own business. Using this industry you can build that kind of business which grows exponentially. Many people will make a fortune by taking advantage of this wave. You and I can be one of them!

If you look in the economic history of humanity you can see how influential the network systems have been and still are on the changes and social evolution. You will find that the basis for the progress of the old Chinese empire was the road and chanel irrigation network. Ancient Greece was based on a developed shipping network. We all know about the Roman roads, about the aqueducts and the sewerage system complexity in the development of the Roman Empire. The expansion of the railway network is related to the expansion of the capitalist system in the nineteenth century.

Looking from past to present, networks are growing fastly. The first transport and communications networks connected from the very beginning hundreds of thousands of people. Several decades later the radio and the television captured millions of users. In just four years since its creation in 1991, World Wide Web system was already used by more than fifty million people.

Recently, we communicate to the world what we think and where we are in social networks, thereby every minute more than two million video clips are viewed on YouTube, seven hundred thousands messages are written on Facebook, there are two hundred thousands Tweets and more than two thousands new check-ins on Forsquare.

If you look around you, you can see that all is connected to a huge global network already. We are driving on the highway network, we are fueling in the gas station network, we are buying food or medicines from the store network or drugstore network, we are talking on the phone in network, we look at TV in network, we get cash from an ATM network and the examples could go almost interminably.

That's how new and countless business opportunities came out, starting with on-line marketing and advertising to network franchising, or network-marketing.

NETWORK MARKETING

BEGINNINGS

In the last hundred years businesses have expanded in an uninterrupted rythm. The Industrial Revolution caused many farmers to migrate to mass production in the new factories. This led to the fast growth of urban population. As a result, the products began to reach consumers through a new distribution and wholesale / retail marketing system. The bigger the towns were, the bigger the stores got. Evolution led to the birth of the first supermarkets and then the big shopping malls.

In the 50's, in the United States, a new concept appeared, called concession or franchise. This demanded a new type of business, basically one that was based on a pre-existing successful project, with a certain price of access. Being something new and perhaps in the desire to protect the status quo, some lawmakers then considered that the franchises / concessions are some kind of pyramid scheme. Even in the United States Congress the elimination of this type of business was claimed, the draft passing forward to a difference of only 11 votes. Now the franchise / concession type of business varies from car sale to financial services, from banking services to doughnut stores, insurance, etc.

At the beginning of the new millennium, however, time has become the most precious merchandise. What was once fun to spend the day shopping is now regarded as a luxury, a waste of time that the modern family can not afford anymore given that most often family members must generate additional revenue to keep pace with the increasingly large cost of modern life.

Lack of time and the need for additional revenue generated a new type of business that is growing vertiginously in a new industry and a new economic wave. It's the modern distribution network based on references, Network Marketing.

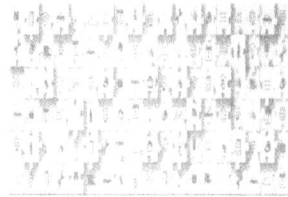

ORIENTATION

Network Marketing or Multi-Level Marketing (MLM) is a legitimate business in which companies pay their distributors for advertising and trade only when their products are sold. Those working in the field receive commission for their activity of placing the products in the market and an original strategy, the outstanding power of advertising is put to work profitably for all participants in the business. Because they don't spend million of dollars for press, radio and television commercial, companies use some of this budget for remunerating distributors' network. These ones come from all backgrounds: simple workers, businessmen, teachers, doctors, etc ... They complete their income through network marketing business.

Although it was born half a century ago, only now we can say that Network Marketing came out of the tough pioneer period, going so far through three stages.

In the first stage, same way as for the concession / franchise, this new system hit the reticence of those who did not understand it. The turnoff from this phase took place in 1979, when the Federal Trade Commission of the United States recognized as legitimate business and not a pyramid one of the largest trading companies* of Multi Level Networking.

The second phase started in the early 80's with the bloom of science and technology development.
Many companies who wanted to exploit the network sale force and new technologies appeared overnight. Unfortunately most of the network distributors that time flinched in front of the new technological waves, not being familiar with them or not having the time to adjust as they were caught between multiple activities starting from the sale process to daily update of the stock and honoring the orders.Today in stage three, the companies in the field use simple and understandable compensation systems using modern technology both for them and distributors, which now, the more advanced it is made the easier to use. For today's network distributor, the company is in charge of tax and customs, stock and logistics and customers can be directed for information and orderes to a telephone service (call center) or web page. This way the network-marketing system gets accesible to a growing number of people. Briefly, the time has never been better. Those who choose this type of business today, are the winners of a major ace in the hole,

*Amway Corporation

because now is the moment when MLM industry embarks on a new and strong stage of development.

If someone would ask you to choose between one hundred thousand Euros - cash or a cent which will double daily for a whole month, what would you choose? I am pretty convinced that the second alternative. Considering that the first doubling of the cent happened on day one, at the end of the thirty one day there will be twenty-one million euros. Interesting ... and it is called geometric progression. Multilevel marketing makes this math power work for your business.

A MLM structure of independent distributors of a national or multinational company usually works like this: a distributor co-opts more people to promote the company's products or services on the market. Once signed up and have themselves become distributors, they are carring out this through a personal marketing / sale of products activity and / or by direct co-optation into the system of a group of people who want to expand at their turn the business by their own subsidiaries and market strategies. Each participant in an MLM business cashes in commissions on registered product turnovers both from personal sales of products and the wide network of coworkers (direct and indirect ones) that he created.

Let's give a hypothetical example. In the first month you recruited five coworkers and in the second month, we presume that each of them recruits let's say another five people and the recruitment continues for six months. This way you will have in your downline (the number of coworkers generated by your efforts and the ones of the team you've created) 19,530 network distributors. If we assume that each person in this group buy goods or services in the amount of one hundred euros per month from the network distribution company and you have a rate of ten percent from each sale, after six months the total commission will be 195.300 EUR. Obviously, this example is very simplified and idealized and no business has the regularity of a Swiss watch, but it was offered for demonstration and vision. Certainly in MLM industry also there is a drop-out rate and not everyone who starts succeeds, but those who have the energy and perseverance in overcoming obstacles will be able to build a sale organization growing in geometric progression. Many have succeeded.

End of safe jobs

The job means employment for decades (as we know now) only in the last half of the century. The generations before the industrial age considered the job as a task that you were hired to perform once. For example, a dressmaker gets the task of making a dress or a blacksmith to work some agricultural tool. Nobody expected their jobs to last for decades and in the end to receive benefits or retiring pensions.

Today, most people are in the employee position. In most cases, they provide work for a fixed salary (linear income) and some are paid by the hour depending on the time spent at work.

Of course, some consultants may earn serious income this way, from hundreds to thousands of euros / hour. The problem is that they depend effectively on being there during that time. If they get sick, for example, they'd better recover quickly because nobody pays "fat" bed rest. The bottom line is that if you work as an employee, you have to jump up immediately at other people's orders. If the boss wants you in his office at six o'clock, you'd better be present. If a client requests a meeting in another city in a day and at a time convenient to him, you pack and you go. It's actually same as in feudal times when the lord decides where you are and what you do every hour of your life. You will never be free if you sell your life hours for a fixed income.

On the other hand, in the early 2000, with the entry into the new information and globalization age, the future specialists and economic analysts have predicted that jobs as we know belong to the past. In the last 10-15 years, millions of people were laid off from corporations. They searched in vain for other safe jobs and comparable wages. If in the past the layoffs were considered a temporary measure to reduce costs, today they have an entirely different reason. Automation replaces human effort cost and companies move their factories depending on legislative facilities and manpower costs. Those who work are often put in the position to change status from employee to independent subcontractor because companies prefer this type of collaboration in order to limit their tax liability, benefit payment and limitation of working hours, etc.

Today cutbacks continue both in fall periods and in the expansion periods. With the reduction of traditional labor force the contingent of people working with collaboration agreements or other types of independent organization, grows fastly.

End of safe retiring pensions

Approximately fifty years ago you had just one way to ensure a comfortable old age. It usually consisted of working your own land to death or to give it to someone on lease.

Currently, baby boom survivors and the ones from the information generation who are aware of the future will have to support on themselves their old age building independent business.

Social security cut their breath daily, world states are gasping with the current pension schemes and in the near future is almost certain that we will not receive any money from the government.
Even those who put their hope in a new plan of management for social security and personal contributions taxes (invested by insurance companies or private funds in bonds and stock shares) can not sit still. Stock excahnges are unpredictable though, however, being both succeses and collapses. A good fall on the stock market and you say goodbye to your retirement. How will we do in the future depends on how quickly we wake up and embrace reality and current changes and on how we prepare our autonomy.

Reccurent residual income

The only kind of income that ensures a true financial independence and a safe financial refuge is recurrent residual income. This is the lever that makes money come continuously and constantly at a period of time after you have finished working. It is the income that music composers, famous singers and best seller authors obtain from royalties, the successful business owners from dividends and real estate investors from rent. It seems continuously and constantly at a period of time after you that ordinary people remained somewhat on the outside ... But apart from the above models there is still a solution close to everyone which is building a multi level network, which is network marketing.

Source: Richard Poe, The fourth wave, Network Marketing in the 21st Century
Publisher: Amaltea, 2002

MOTIVATIONS

One of the studies conducted by WFDSA in countries where network-marketing organizations exist revealed the most common reasons why people choose this activity:
• It is a good way to know and relate to other people;
• Earnings are equally to the effort;
• Provides a flexible work schedule;
• It is a gainful lucrative activity for additional revenue;
• It is a good way to start a personal business;
• No specific level of education, experience, financial resources or physical condition is needed;
• People of all ages and from all social classes have been successful in this field;
• You can define your own goals and how you will achieve them.

Network-marketing as a concept of operation is based on the following principles: independence, globalization, equal opportunities and last but not least inner motivation to succeed. More by token this industry pays so well!

Currently there are a few basic methods used in marketing for placing products from the producer to the final consumer, namely:

Retailing*
It is the method with which everyone is familiar and in which a customer can buy a product directly from the shelf or from the seller in the business unit. Most present examples are grocery stores, drugstores, food markets, department stores, etc.

Direct Selling*
Direct selling means selling goods and services directly to the consumer through an explanation and / or demonstration at his home or other people's home, at work or in other places away from the retail location. Many countries use the term „home selling" instead of "direct selling".
Direct selling is used for many products and services: certain types of insurance, cosmetics, home tools, fitness products, textiles, jewelry, etc.

Direct mail sales*

Also into the category of direct sales are the mail order ore the direct Internet one (online sales). The latter are currently some of the most popular ways to get revenue and are profitable inasmuch it reaches the target audience effectively.

Online direct sales are gaining more ground than traditional shopping, as there is willingness to buy non-stop, avoid crowds and the prices are lower than in traditional stores because there are no expenses related to rent and employees. Online we can review each product and can read various opinions and recommendations about it. The choice and the variety are unlimited.

Network-marketing

Is the subject of this book and is considered to be the most progressive distribution system because it uses both the power of the distributors' network and the power of trade and online communication. It is a natural reaction of the general globalization in the world. Companies using this system, instead of investing lots of money in expensive advertising, wholesales and deposits, share this money to people who have built or are building consumer networks.

It is at the moment one of the most important business in the world, at which millions of people directly take part and achieve annually sales of hundreds of billions of dollars. In less than half a century, Network Marketing has been proclaimed the next millennium business.

Source: *Don Failla, 45 Second Presentation That Will Change Your Life
Publisher: Digital Data Cluj, 2004

The yesterday unknown is the tomorrow truth" - Nicolas Camille Flammarion

Out of ignorance or prejudice starting from some illegal situations in the past, but which have no connection with network-marketing, some erroneous judgements have been created and spread, such as:

BUIDING NETWORKS IS THE SAME AS PYRAMID SCHEMES
(OR PYRAMIDAL FINANCIAL GAMES)

Pyramid schemes have as background the Ponzi scheme. This pyramid system was named by Charles Ponzi, who in the early 20's cheated thousands of people in New England, convincing them to invest in a speculation scheme with postal stamps. At that time the annual rate of interest for bank accounts was 5%. Ponzi promised that he could provide a 50% profit in just 90 days. First, Ponzi brought some international postal coupons, in order to back up his scheme but, soon he began to pay the first investors from the amounts lodged by the most recent investors.

These schemes are illegal procedures of gain, virtually built as a pyramid or pyramid structure in which the layers (levels) of the pyramid are made up of people who pay a certain amount for entering into the scheme.

The general rule of winning is very simple: people who reach the top of the pyramid can only earn money if lots of people enter the bottom of the scheme. Each person must pay an entrance fee, and then he is required to recruit other people who also have to pay the entrance fee. Their gain consists of the amount of entrance tax from people at the bottom.

So people entering at the bottom of the pyramid give money to a few people who are on top. Each new participant pays for the chance to reach the top and to make profit from the payments of those who will come into the game later. These winning pyramid schemes are also called "mutual aid games" or "closed common funds" or „closed finance and investment clubs", etc.

According to Wikipedia, there is a large common confusion between Ponzi schemes (illegal) and MLM business (sale of products or services in MLM system, legally regulated) because of the similar recommendation system. In the first case it is a recruitment system of some payers (investors) whose operation depends on entering the system larger and larger amounts.

For MLM, it is recommendation marketing through which on a similar structure, products or services are being sold, the resulting amounts being distributed following each company's own algorithm. Unlike the first case, in MLM there is a real commercial system, legal and functional. There are known many MLM companies operating successfully for decades.

In the network-marketing industry, the money come exclusevely from the sale of products or services while in the pyramid schemes money only come from recruiting new members.

THOSE STARTING A NETWORK MARKETING BUSINESS WANT TO GET RICH ON THE ACCOUNT OF THOSE DTARTING AFTER THEM IN THE SAME COMPANY (ONLY THOSE IN THE TOP MAKE MONEY)

In order to clarify, you have to think that everything we know seems like a pyramid: church, state, army, multinational companies, etc.

If we take for example a multinational company, the organizational structure will look like this:

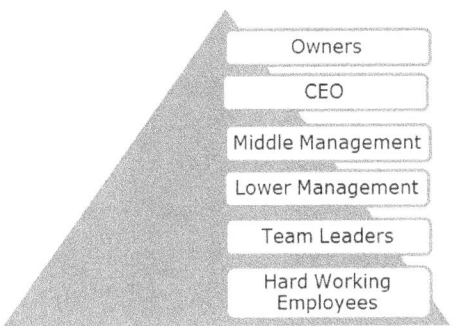

It is clearly a pyramid scheme. The question is what chance the ones on the last level have to earn more than those on the interrmediate levels above them. If we refer to a MLM as a pyramid structure, which runs on six depths of payment, and each independent distributor (on any depth) has access to recurrent residual revenue of 5% in the six paid depths, the situation looks like this:

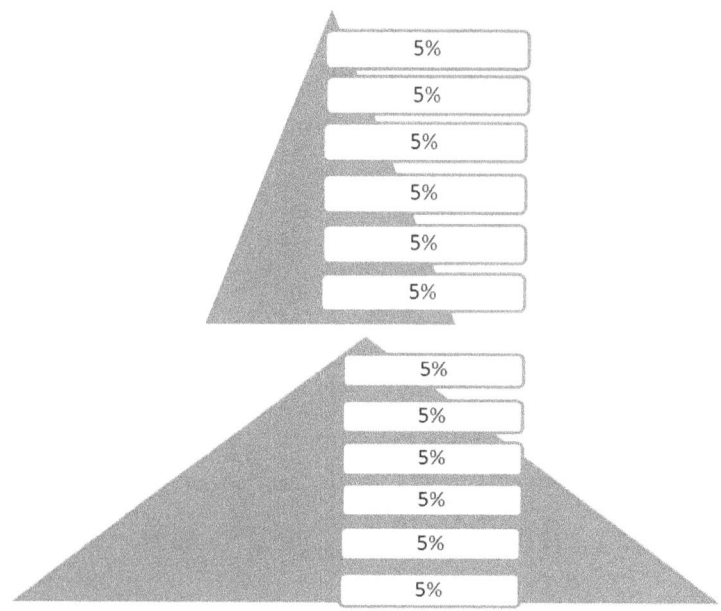

What people don't know is that in general, the MLM companies' business plans give you access to each payment depth, only when you build the necessary width or the right proportion (in the binary system).

Such a structure could look like:

Depth	1	2	3	4	5	6
1	5%					
2		5%				
3			5%			
4				5%		
5					5%	
6						5%

Or it may look like this - if we refer to the binary system (that is, the formation of two teams generating volumes). This system pays the balance to infinity ... but limited weekly to a certain percentage.

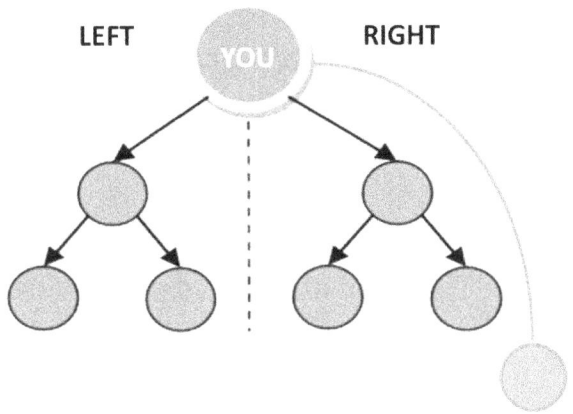

Let's say, for example, that the team on the left generated a $ 4,000 sales volume in a week, and the right-hand team raised another $ 5,000. Percentage of payment to say is 10%

Or it may look like this - if we refer to the binary system (that is, the formation of two teams generating volumes). This system pays the balance to infinity ... but limited weekly to a certain percentage.

How does this balance work? It's very simple ... the equivalent volume for both teams is $ 4,000, which means you are paid this week with 10% of $ 4,000 - that's $ 400. But will stay in balance for the next week of pay - $ 1000 on the right side. It is a system to which everybody always contributes, the one who came first and the one who came last.

This system is made to function on the principle of equality, where the one in the last depth, can build even long after the one who first started the business, an organization to generate much larger turnovers of products and services, so more consistent commissions than the one above him.

Here, everyone will reach a payment level in accordance with his merits. This is an ethical system that rewards hard work and perseverance, sustainable achievements.

WILL BE TRULY SUCCESSFUL ONLY THOSE WHO REGISTER FIRST IN A NEW-ESTABLISHED COMPANY

There are certain advantages and disadvantages if you start at the beginning, same as if you start later. The facts show that there are successful people who started with a particular company when it launched, and there are successful people who started much later with the same company and have themselves become successful.

However, it seems better to get affiliated with a company which has more time and big turnovers in the back. The infrastructure is already at hand, the products are already known in the market and the confidence level is high. On the other hand, many companies starting in their pioneering period collapse after a few years or are being sold. But those who resist and remain after the five to ten years threshold, probably provide to those who started a revolutionary and sustainable business plan and / or cutting edge products and technologies that compensate for the lack of decades of experience, the advantage of the older ones in the industry.

99% OF THOSE WHO MAKE NETWORK-MARKETING ARE AGGRESIVE SELLERS AND I AM NOT GOING TO DO ANYTHING LIKE THIS EVER

The truth is that also in building this type of business, as in many others, 90% of the people are amateurs without the proper training, who think they can give a quick shot and get rich fast.

If you judge on a large scale, that someone met or heard in the last ten years a network builder each year and nine of the ten were amateurs, the acumulated experience is that they are all amateurs.
But in classic business the very same thing happens, which is why most of them fail, on average after the first five years. Negative generalizations can be eyed in any field such that all doctors take bribes, all lawyers are liars and persuasives, all athletes are illiterate, etc.

The final truth is that in this business, as in any other one, there is the mass of the ones with less knowledge and the narrower crowd of professionals. It is therefore our duty to do our business professionally and thus to dismantle by personal example all these false concepts that goes unfairly with network-marketing.

PART II BUILDER GUIDANCE SYSTEM

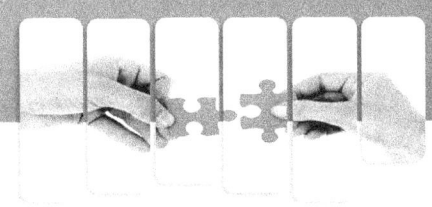

PART II
MLM NETWORK BUILDER GUIDANCE SYSTEM

It was created so that anyone can acquire the necessary skills to be effective in building a network-marketing business.

It is a guidance system designed to help those who intend to become professionals in this industry and an easy way to understand where you are now and what you need to help you achieve your goals.

In conclusion, this system aims to constitute itself as a simple and practical tool to start your own business. You will find out further which steps you need to follow in order to build a stable and big business. The key is actually in seven principles which are the success recipe for building any multi-level network business.

These are:

1. **SETTING THE TARGETS;**
2. **MAKING AND MAINTAINING A LIST OF NAMES;**
3. **HOW TO INVITE LIKE A PROFESSIONAL;**
4. **PRESENTING THE OPPORTUNITY;**
5. **SECOND MEETING / FINALIZING THE FIRST MEETING;**
6. **PROFESSIONAL START (BUSINESS INITIATION);**
7. **TEAMWORK PROCESS.**

In addition to these seven principles, as helping tools it is desired to read books, listen to professional CDs and DVDs. Professionals use all events organized by the company or by the guidance system (open, workshop, regional and international conference).

This working tools not only help in your work but they are also compressing the time spent for building the business and they are working for you even when you are not present (for example, a DVD or an event can inform and motivate more people in the same time).

All this taken together are designed as a "turnkey" guidance system and systematic following of such a system has proven to be the most effective and fast way to build a stable network.

1. SETTING THE TARGETS (GOALS)

"A goal is a dream with a deadline" - Napoleon Hill

To illustrate the importance of setting goals, I'll give you a very suggestive example from the literature: in "Alice in Wonderland" at some point in her journey, Alice reaches a crossroads where she meets a clever cat. And she asks the cat what way she should take, which of the roads. And the cat replied with a question: where do you want to get to? Well, I do not know! ... Alice answered. Then take any road you want, it does not matter anyway, said the cat.

The bottom line is that you'll never get where you want, without knowing which the destination is. Most people don't set a destination, don't set goals. They are constantly searching for something, constantly waiting for something and are most often in one of these two situations:

• Some have a state of discontent and feel unhappy. They feel like they have abandoned their ideals and the life they have dreamed of someday. They don't know what to do;

• Others feel they can do more. They want more clarity and structure to fulfill their dreams. They don't know how to do it.

And still, why is that the big majority of people in the two categories above do not set or write goals?

• Because they don't know exactly what goals mean. Most think that they have already set goals, when in fact it's just the desires and expectations, such as "I want to be rich","I want to have money", "I want to be fulfilled" or "I want a beautiful life". The idea is these are not goals for sure. There are simple fantasies and unclear desires, common to all men;

• Because people don't believe and don't know that setting goals is important.

If the majority of people grow up in a society where hardly anyone has defined goals or valueing them whatsoever, they will reach adulthood without knowing that the knowledge to set goals has more effect on their lives than anything else.

• Because people don't know their potential.

Man is great. We all have within us the ability to achieve almost any target we propose. The greatest responsibility we have to ourselves is to clearly know what we want and how to achieve it.

As clearer the goals are, the more we will unleash the latent potential within us and we will achieve them. It is now known that a person uses only 2% of its mental potential. What remains stays in reserve waiting to be used someday.

It's like receiving an inheritance of 1 million euros and you would only know how to use your entire life only 20,000...

If we really know what we want, our mind will take us from where we are to where we want to go. A dream turns into goal from the moment we feel called by it and we act.
First it is necessary to distinguish between what a dream is and what a palpable goal is. The dream is always something general, it can be an idea or a wish, but only with a clear configuration it will become a goal. For example, if you want to be rich and famous, this is a dream that can become a goal if you know clearly in what field you want to gain reputation, when and what benefits it will bring you. And it will become true, if you have the mental map of the road that you have to go on to get where you want to go.

In order to be powerful goals should be written. The fact that you write them will make your subconscious start working and looking for opportunities to achieve them. Scientific studies have shown that man retains only 10% of the information he finds out, and the remaining 90% is stored in subconscious, waiting for someday to be used.

So, even if you forget, your subconscious will not forget and will always seek for ways.

Why have goals? To have a direction! People who do not have specific targets but only desires and dreams, most likely will remain only with the dreams.

Write your goals in a notebook and your mind will train and focus on what you actually want and not on what you are just dreaming to happen in your life. Moreover, if you regularly read your goals and you visualise them whenever you feel to, the picture of the life you desire will be alive in your mind and this will motivate you not to stray from your path.

Here are some suggestions on how to formulate and organize your goals (they must cover all sides of your life):

• Faith;
• Health / fettle;
• House (family);
• Close friends;
• Wealth;
• Activity;
• Entertainment (fun, hobbies).

They must be:

1. Written on paper (a notebook for targets / goals);
2. Specific and set for an orientative period of time;

3. Formulated with confidence, write what you truly want;
4. To answer the following questions:
• Why do I need to really feel good?
• How will I become better by achieving this goal?
• What will I give back directly and indirectly?
• What will be the price I will pay?
• Why do I want this? (Specify minimum 10 reasons, the more the better. If you have sufficient reasons you can accomplish anything)

5. To be measurable.
Here is an example of a notebook for goals:

	FAITH		
	Spirituality	Personal Development	Fears to face
		Books Audiobooks Seminars	
1			
2			
3			
4			
5			

	HEALTH		
	type of food	exercise / sports	Features
1			
2			
3			
4			
5			

	RELATIONS			
	Family		**Friends**	
	Communication	Time spent together	Communication	Time spent together
1				
2				
3				
4				
5				

	WEALTH		
	Possessions	Financial success	Business
1			
2			
3			
4			
5			

	ACTIVITY				
	Business / Job	Skills to teach	Things to create	Things to finish	New skills
1					
2					
3					
4					
5					

	ENTERTAINMENT			
	Places to visit	Adventure	Hobby	Fun
1				
2				
3				
4				
5				

	Why	How	Since when/ until when
1			
2			
3			
4			
5			

For each of the activities listed above, organize yourself as follows:

	Why	How	Since when/ until when
1			
2			
3			
4			
5			

The list of goals must be read with enthusiasm and passion every day. Live what you read, give life to your goals in your mind.

And it is very important that they belong to you, to firmly believe in them and to really want them.

Some people get quickly to what they want, others remain disappointed a lifetime. You too have such people around you. How big your achievements are depends heavily on how much you believe in your goals. The secret is to stay committed to your goals and to keep your inner motivation even when you encounter obstacles and challenges.

In conclusion, reinvent your mind and make yourself a daily habit from setting and achieving your goals.

The most useful tool you have when building a multi-level network is your list of names. From this list some people will become your partners and other people clients. The good news is that it is an asset that can be expanded again and again.

What is essential about the list of names?
• It must be accessible and easy to handle;
• You should always extend it;
• It is more than a "list of names".

ACCESIBLE AND EASY TO HANDLE:
The basic rule is that it must be written (not in mind) on paper, in your workbook or on cards in alphapetical order. The advice is to number people names in order for you to always know how you position yourself.

The access to the list must be simple both for yourself and for your coworkers.

ALWAYS MUST BE EXTENDED:

If you don't have new prospects, the list will end at some

moment and you will have no one to talk about the opportunity or the products. Therefore, you will not have a business.

And because your business' growth depends on the number of people that find out the information from you, it is essential that every day you have new prospects that get in your list.

IS MORE THAN A "LIST OF NAMES"
The list of names, contrary to the term, it is not a sequence of names and phone numbers. It includes also observations about each person (eg businessman, diabetic, works or has worked in MLM, has relationships in the medical field, the aunt is a salewoman, boyfriend is director of a clinic, etc.)

The most important informations that can be "the trigger" for the person on your list and give you a good tactical position are:

• How many years does he/she have?
• What does he/she do?
• What it is his/her position?
• What are his/her circumstances?
• What hobbies does he/she have?

The next step is to organize the list on target groups in order to generate results in the most effective and fast way:

Group 1: family and friends
Usually they are the first to find out the information from you and become the first customers. They are on the hot list.

Group 2: aquaintances
They are those with whom you have had contact in the past and if you call them and introduce yourself, they know who you are. It's the warm list.

Group 3: top 20
These people are your "powerful" market and they are those with position and influence, opinion leaders in their field or community. From them you can get excellent recommandation and they will be product consumers, their influence will make a great ad. On the other hand, if they begin to build the network, at the first call they will manage to mobilize lots of people.

Group 4: recommendations
They are those people who you have not met in person, but that one of the above groups recommended as potential clients or open for discussion. They are also called cold list, but statistics show that over eighty percent of your business will be built with these people.

Examples of how we ask for recommendations:

• Do you know someone who has initiative and is open to new?

• Do you know anyone who wants an additional income?
• Do you know anyone who has lost his job and wants to make money?
• Do you know anyone who wants to start a business?
• Etc.

Interestingly, there are many cases when we put such questions and even the questioned person will respond "I myself am interested".

Or, when you get refusals, you can use the following example in order to get recommendations:

"I understand perfectly your reasons and maybe it is not the right time for you to start this business. However, as the market grows from day to day, it would be a shame to lose the chance. Certainly your friends, colleagues, aquaintaces, relatives will be contacted by someone with this business proposal. Therefore, for you to win something from your portfolio of relationships here is how we can do: we can now make together a list of people (from your phone) that I will approach in a professional manner. Many people are interested in an additional income. The first person of those recommended by you who decides to buy products or to start the business, I'll let you know immediately. This way I work for you, with your people, without you spending time or money to invest. Meanwhile, after you'll see that you already have partners, if you want, you can also do this business."

Example of how we build the list of names:

	Who	Name / Surname
1.	Mother	
2.	Father	
3.	Brother	
4.	Sister	
5.	Grandfather A	
6.	Grandmother A	
7.	Grandfather B	
8.	Grandmother B	
9.	Mother-in-law	
10.	Father-in-law	
11.	Godfather	
12.	Godmother	
13.	Brother-in-law	
14.	Sister-in-law	
15.	Cousin A	
16.	Girl cousin A	
17.	Cousin B	
18.	Girl cousin B	
19.	Aunt A	
20.	Uncle A	
21.	Aunt B	
22.	Uncle B	

23.	Daughter-in-law
24.	Son-in-law
25.	Best friend
26.	Best friend's wife
27.	Friend 1
28.	Friend 2
29.	Friend 3
30.	Friend 4
31.	Friend 5
32.	Friend 6
33.	Friend 7
34.	Friend 8
35.	Friend 9
36.	Friend 10
37.	Friend 11
38.	Friend 12
39.	Friend 13
40.	Friend 14
41.	Friend 15
42.	Friend 16
43.	Friend 17
44.	Friend 18
45.	Friend 19
46.	Friend 20
47.	Ex-

	girlfriend/boyfriend
48.	Ex-wife/husband
49.	Middle school deskmate
50.	Highschool deskmate
51.	Middle school classmate
52.	Middle school girl classmate
53.	College mate 1
54.	College mate 2
55.	College girl mate 1
56.	College girl mate 2
57.	School governess
58.	Middle school Class teacher
59.	Highschool Class teacher
60.	Favourite college teacher
61.	Favourite college female teacher
62.	Neighbour 1
63.	Neighbour 2
64.	Female Neighbour 1

65.	Female Neighbour 2
66.	Building janitor
67.	Workfellow
68.	Female workfellow
69.	Wife's workfellow
70.	Wife's female workfellow
71.	Ex-workfellow
72.	Ex-female workfellow
73.	Parents at child's school
74.	Child's governess
75.	Child's coach
76.	Your coach
77.	Salesman from whom you bought the car
78.	The insurer
79.	Your client
80.	Your boss
81.	Your ex-boss
82.	Your wife's boss
83.	Your wife's ex-boss
84.	The pharmacist
85.	The accountant
86.	The banker managing

your accounts	
87.	The driving teacher
88.	The car mechanic
89.	The priest
90.	The priest's wife
91.	The electrician
92.	The real estate agent
93.	The barber
94.	The hair dresser
95.	The manicure lady
96.	The vet
97.	The posteman
98.	The family doctor
99.	The gynecologist
100.	The dentist

This is just an example. The list can be extended much more if you ask yourself the proper questions such as – do I know anybody who: is a fitness instructor, goes training with me, is a salesman, sales credits, has recently closed his firm, wants a business, etc. After completing the list with 100 – 200 persons, you pass to the detailed list:

Nr.	Name	Phone	Group	Ocupation	Motivation	Details	First meeting	Event	Follow Up
1									
2									
3									
4									
5									
6									
7									
8									
9									
10									

I suggest you to also write those whom you deliberately omitted because you think they are not interested in the products or that they will never build a network. I cannot describe the feeling when you get a sight of a person you know, whom you did not call intentionally and that person is someone else's guest at the event for building the business that you also participate at...

Now, at the end, think about the fact that you have not even known your lover before you met her / him.

The invitation is the first direct contact with the person on the name list, with your potential partner. The purpose of the invitation is that the person you're talking with to meet you in order to present him the information about your business.

To have a high rate of confirmations:

• It is preferred that you make the invitation by phone with determination but without pushing. In the end, the invitation's success depends on the attitude;
• Is brief and to the point, so it lasts no more than three minutes and targets fixing a meeting;
• Is sincerely enthusiastic;
• Is personalized – you adapt your speech to each interlocutor.

The professionals follow four steps:

1. Make somehow so your prospect be as positive as posible

When people are emotionally positive, they will always be open and receptive. You can't know in advance how the person's you are going to call state of spirit is, but you can bring or maintain it to a positive level if:

• you make a sincere compliment,
• you are friendly and you smile (it feels and is transmitted also by phone).

2. Make him/her curious

Give him information so that is not too much and make him believe that he has understood from a few words, but enough to create interest and to move on.

3. Control the direction of the discussion and the level of information

Because you have done well at the second point, it is now inevitable for questions not to run. Never forget that your goal is to awaken interest, but not to do the summary of your business on the phone. It's about business and money and details are given only face to face. If someone insists with questions you have the handy solution - the word "obvious." Almost all people think that they are good at everything and their ego determines them not to accept otherwise. If you say "obviously it is not a topic to be discussed on the phone, isn't it?" the questions will not want to be in contradiction with this indisputable principle.

You do not make a summary on the phone because you want to give your prospect the information in person and personalized, so he will decide based on a more complete and accurate documentation. At first glance your business can resemble many negative things that people have heard, such as pilot games, pyramid games or door to door sale and they can take unaware hasty decisions. Therefore it is better to be in control during the phone conversation.

4. Ask for reliability
The decisive step is to set a palpable meeting. The rule is to propose two terms from which the prospect will finally choose one, actually choosing between two "yes".

At this point it is important to check if the details of the meeting are noted: "I wrote in my workbook, we meet Thursday at 5:15 p.m. at my working point from 7-9, Dorobanți. Please write down as well and if something happens, let me know in advance. I have another important meeting set after you and time is extremely precious because I want to give you the complete information".

The invitation must be personalized, adapted to the individual and to the context. It must not be standard and also not to be too much like any other invitation used in our field, because our business must not be associated with another one in the field and the discussion to get an unwanted direction. The invitation will be made so that the approached person thinks about a business like any other one and about the possibility of making money.

Your attitude should indicate that you are in the position to provide something useful and helpful, and you are only asking for seriousness. The perfect invitation is the one that ends up with your prospect having a good feeling after hanging up and with the suspense to participate in a discussion of which he has everything to gain.

Models of invitations:
Friends:

You: Hey buddy, pay attention why I'm calling you. We definitely need to meet because I recently started a business and I want you to know what it is about, I'm sure that it will interest you!

Him: Well, what is it? Tell me on the phone!

You: We've known each other for so long, there's not something to talk on the phone and much more than that I want you to meet my business partner. When can we meet: today or tomorrow?

Him: Tomorrow.

You: Okay, at 5:00 p.m or at 7:00 p.m.?

Him: 7:00 p.m.

You: Okay, I noted the hour; write down yourself also because my partner will come there especially for you!

Him: Ok, I noted, it's settled.

Acquaintances:

You: Hello Mr. Ionescu. D. B. on the phone. Do you have two minutes?

He: Yes.

You: Here is why I called you (you do not ask how he is doing, there is a risk that the discussion goes in another direction and takes longer that it should); I recently started a turnkey business and I place products and technologies with monopoly status in the industry I activate. I'm also focusing on the development of this turnkey business network in our area. Because I know you to be a reliable man and open to new ideas, I consider that you would also be interested to know details!

Him: Okay, and what should I do?

You: I am looking for 2-3 partners with whom to develop this business and I am convinced that you are a person with great potential. When can we meet to show you the business plan: tomorrow or the day after tomorrow?

Him: Tomorrow would be ok;

You: Good, at 5:00 p.m or 7:00 p.m?

Him: At 7:00 p.m;

You: It's very good at 7:00 p.m, because we will have the opportunity to discuss also with my business partner, you will get a complete information. I noted in my workbook, I understand that you did too;

He: Yes, just now. We will meet tomorrow.

Recommandations:
You: Hello, Mr. Moore?

Him: Yes, that's me;

You: D. B. is my name and we haven't personnaly met each other yet. I am calling you on behalf of Mrs Jackson. Do you know her?

He: Of course!

You: Okay, here is why I'm calling you. I own the rights to a turnkey business for our area. In a discussion that I had with Mrs Jackson, she warmly recommended your person, as a very dynamic personality, open-minded so this is why I am calling you; I practically introduce in our country products and technologies that internationally are monopolies but I'm also placing the rights for this turnkey business. Where can we see each other for 30 minutes to show you the business plan and the technologies: tomorrow or the day after tomorrow?

Him: You know, I'm a very busy person and I'd rather have you sending me the information about this business on e-mail before we meet;

You: Yes, I understand and I believe that you are indeed a busy person, me too. That is why we really need to talk. It would be TOTALLY unprofessional of me to send you the information about the business on email. It is a new concept and frankly, we have to meet before I send the specific information on email.

When do you have 30 minutes to spare: tomorrow or the day after tomorrow?

Him: The day after tomorrow;

You: Okay, the day after tomorrow it is, in the morning or the afternoon?

Him: In the afternoon, after 5:00 p.m;

You: For me it would be perfect at 6.30 p.m. or 7:00 p.m.;

Him: 6:30 p.m. is okay;

You: Well, I already noted in my workbook 6:00 p.m., the day after tomorrow. Need I remind you of our meeting the morning the day after tomorrow or have you also noted yourself?

Him: Yeah, I noted, there is no need for confirmation.

You: All the best then and I will see you the day after tomorrow. I can't wait to get to know you in person!

- If the person insists to know more details then we can tell him (depending on the specific of the business) for example:

-

Sir, these technologies with a monopoly position are in the (for example) nutrition, genetics and wellness: health, antiaging, the most dynamic trend in the world at the moment. I'm looking for 2-3 serious partners with whom to develop this business to a much higher level, and you are a person who deserves to know this information. Obviously we can't talk on the phone about technologies and money!

Ok, I understand.

Then the time and the place for the meeting are clearly set.

WHAT NOT TO DO WHEN INVITING

Experts say that a phone call can be thrown away in two ways: if you talk too much or talk too little.

In the first case, you fall into the trap of boring the speaker or making the presentation on the phone;In the second case, you will say a few generalities, you will stumble and ultimately in the happiest case you will transmit insecurity and in the most unfortunate case you will not get any meeting either.

Preparing the meeting

The first meeting is the first direct "confrontation" between you and the prospect. The first basic things that you must take care in a professional manner are the conditions to conduct the meeting. Your outfit will have be as for a businessman, the presentation place will have a "business air" without disturbing factors (loud music, cell phones, background noises, too hot or too cold, etc).

Before the meeting you must analyze (once again) all that you know about the one that you will have the meeting with:

what he does for a living, what would be his motivation and then, during the discussion it will get easier for you to know what kind of issue he is seeking solutions for. In this manner, you will focus on presenting the business opportunity or presenting certain products.

Things you need: time table for scheduling meetings, a notebook size A4 wove paper, a presentation catalogue, infoDVD, magazines, a book about the concept of network-marketing business, a contract in paper.

First impression

Even if you realize it or not, we all make a first impression about those we are meeting for the first time, usually within 30 seconds. This first impression gives you the feeling of sympathy or antipathy for that person. Thoughts like "he is a bit like me," "he is not at all like me," "he is like George" etc. are generated.

Be aware that you create the first impression. It is transmitted by your way of communicating with the ones around you. Generally, people communicate in three ways: through the words they use, through the voice used for saying those words: volume, speed, tempo and power; however, in an overwhelming proportion of 70-85%, people communicate non-verbally, through gestures, facial expressions and posture.

Effective Communication

• Direct your body's position towards your speaker or get close to him. When a person says something interesting, in order to show that you are excited about the subject;

• Use facial expressions. Whenever someone tells you something that surprises you or cheers you, show that using various facial expressions;

• Gesture. When you're curious about a particular issue or you want to approve something, use your body movements and hands to make gestures that indicate these things;

• Approve by head movements. When you want to show the person you're talking to that you agree with what he/she says, approve by slight movements of the head forward. Also, you can move your head left and right to indicate disapproval;

• Keep eye contact during about two-thirds of the discussion. Look your speaker in the eyes, this will show him that you are listening and you're paying attention to him. Eye contact is intended to establish a trustful relationship between people communicating;

• Smile! When you communicate with someone, smile is the element that helps the most to empathize with your speaker. But make sure you smile only when necessary.

The technic of sitting down at the discussion table *

With regard to the discussion table position, strategic arrangement is an effective way to earn your speaker's cooperation. The position in which a person sits to you is showing how he relates to you.

For business meetings or "half an hour" calls, square table is usually used. Technically, the disposal may be:

• Corner position (recommended for first 1:1meeting)

When two people sit in this position they will gladly converse, will have a friendly and spontaneous communication. The position provides them the opportunity to look into each other's eyes, to gesture and to observe the other one's gestures. The corner of the table is only a partial block and gives each person his own space.

Technically speaking, in most cases, it is preferable that the prospect sits on your right simply because it is easier for him to see what you are writing down.

• Cooperation position

This is the one where two persons are sitting on the same side of the table.

It's usually when people think alike or work on the same task. It is one of the most favorable positions to gain your companion's acceptance (can be used successfully at the second meeting, the one for finalization, before signing the contract).

• Competitive-defensive position (to be avoided)

When people are positioned like this, unconsciously they divide the table in two equal areas. Thus each of them will defend his area and will mark it using the objects on the table, will move the time table, pen or phone.

Sitting across the table, face to face, will result in an atmosphere of competition or defensive.
People sitting in this position are infexibile in accepting their companion's opinion and will strongly support their points of view. The table will be a solid impediment, conversations will be short, concise and to the point.

The characteristics of a presentation

A good presentation lasts no more than half an hour, from which five to ten minutes you should discuss formalities with your prospect, listen him and encourage him to talk. You will surely notice how a mutual trust is built, based on a feeling of sympathy. An open dialogue will follow, a truly "verbal ballet" from which it will come out victorious open communication between two people and building a relationship of trust.

In general terms, the meeting should be both informational, to communicate your arguments clearly and logically, and in the same time enthusiastic and personal, so that your prospect gains vision and enthusiasm, seeing himself making this type of business. Last but not least, what you present must be duplicable and easy to use for your disciples and your future prospects.

• With contagious enthusiasm

It is known that you have to burn if you want to go off like a rocket. You'll be able to induce enthusiasm to your prospect only if you have it and you provide the information as such. Enthusiasm means firm commitment and positive attitude. Your energy will transcend your words and the accuracy of the information. Your enthusiasm and energy is 80% of the presentation's success. The prospect will catch the first impression you make and the energy you transmit.

• How to pass the information

What you need to follow when you make a presentation is to be balanced. If you're too short, usually you will not be able to describe what you offer. If the presentation is too long, you will give too many details, you will answer too many questions and you will make the impression to the one standing in front of you that he is not able or doesn't have time for all that. Besides that, if you don't leave some questions unanswered, the magic disappears and also the chance to complete the discussion on a second meeting.

Ideally, your presentation should be:

1. Logic, with beginning-middle-end and sustained with arguments;

2. To present solutions rather than products (eventually it will go on arguing problem-problem's solution); you can come up with solutions to problems such as: lack of money, lack of time, illness, aging, etc.

3. Will leave behind some unanswered questions. Experts say that you did a good presentation if although apparently you gave all the information to the person in front of you it is necessary for him to meet you again. And he wants this to happen quickly.

Duplicable

Why? So that the way you pass the information to be learned and passed on to those in your team, who will be different as temperament, training, intelligence, etc. Remember that it doesn't matter what works just for you. Here it matters what can be duplicated in your team.

*Source: Allan Pease, Body Language
Polimark Publishing House, Bucharest, 1993

Your target

To have a business discussion that targets to help the prospect in making a positive decision, so that he realizes that you are there to help him and to support him to use the new information or products in order for him to have a better life in the future. The final target is that your prospect joins your business and stays with the good feeling that he took the right decision.

What is *"finalisation"*?
If the person invited has not decided "yes" or "no" on the first 1:1 meeting, then you need to have a second meeting. In this situation, you must settle a new meeting in the next 48 hours. The more time passes, the less chance of receiving a positive signal from your prospect, because people tend to pay attention to present things, perhaps less important, but that will draw them away from the enthusiasm left by your meeting.

The second meeting is often a mental and emotional "chess game", the point where your prospect decides whether he will become your partner or your client. This discussion is actually a negotiation and starts from the fact that each of you has needs and direct or indirect interests that you want to meet after this discussion.

What should you look for?

Your most important targets are to identify and correctly formulate the prospect's vital needs. These needs will be, at all stages of discussion, the speaker's motivation for negotiation. Then you will focus on solving the needs, on the advantages and benefits that will come from your partnership. In this regard, all the real advantages that he will have after accepting the offer should be identified and exposed. Usually, next steps are: answering objections and then taking the decision.

What you must do*

Finalizing a "sale" means communication and negotiation throughout the discussions and eventually creating a relationship after sale, through your services.
You must create a relationship of agreement and understanding in order to reach "the same wavelength." You will get this agreement using three principles of buiding an effective communication: calibration, mirroring and leadership.

Calibration consists in observing and recognizing the interlocutor's emotional state. You will gather this way information on his ability to receive information and accept the deal. This process is very important because the emotional state of both participants in discussion is essential.

Mirroring is the next part of the communication process and is referring at you observing the prospect's physical behavior and language. In this phase, for establishing a strong connection with the one in front of you, you must mirror his posture, tone of voice and gestures. You will then create a climate of mutual trust, because people tend to have sympathy for those who are alike. Mirroring will give you the feeling that you have something in common, that you behave and think the same.

Leadership is the process to decode the signal you receive from your negotiation partner and to influence and guide the discussion and how will the sale close in relation to what you want, but respecting your prospect's options.

It is vital that you don't do all the work during the transaction process. If your prospect will be just passive, it will be difficult to mobilize and agree finalizing the transaction. Too many people in sales believe that everything depends on them, when in fact the secret is to make your prospect involve increasingly, until the decision of closing the deal is already a certainty.

In conclusion, finalizing the negotiation or the sale is a complex thing that will require mostly empathizing with the man in front of you, to find out his false objections and to communicate him that you want to make the deal, both for you and for him. It's the positive attitude and not the mentality of the winner (as certain sales courses teach) that should be followed throughout the presentation – closing the sale. At the end of the transaction we don't find a winner and a loser. You will know that you have been successful if at the end you will shake hands and smile with a "win-win" mutual feeling.

Answering objections

These should be considered natural aspects for a negotiation or sale. Remember how many times you personally said you don't need to buy, or you don't have time to start a project that was presented to you, but eventually you bought that thing or you started the project. That happened because the one who made the sale was able to overcome objections in a professional manner. When you encounter an objection it doesn't mean that the sale or negotiation will not end positively, it means that the interlocutor, customer, prospect, needs your help in making a decision which satisfies him emotionally.

†Source: http://www.nlp-evolutiv.ro/vanzari/vanzari-cu-rapport

There are cases in which the prospect has a real objection and a response to the point is the most appropriate strategy. But usually people avoid telling their real objections and they throw out those reasons that they think they sound well. It's a real skill to answer an objection in a constructive way, so as to start a sale / negotiation successfully, especially because people often get to buy exactly for the same reason for which they had initially refused the sale raising the objection.

For prospects objections are some kind of true or false defense systems, but for you they are opportunities to discover new needs and interests of the one you are talking with.

Objections usually hide one or more of the following six reasons:

1. He didn't understand something
It is necessary for you have to find out what he did not understand and you can do that by repeating the information process' steps as long as necessary, until you're convinced that things are clear;

2. He doesn't belive
He doesn't think he can win the money you have shown him that this type of business can bring or he doesn't believe that the product is exactly what you said or that you will help him (that it's all about teamwork). This is simple, show him the evidences;

3. Wants to test the market first
He wants to talk to people around him, relatives or friends. He clearly didn't understand what it's about and you obviously
have to come back in fact to reason number 1. Explain that if he's not involved and doesn't control the elements of the business as a professional, then he can't ask advice from "experts" who haven't even heard the information. Explain that people have opinions about everything, even if they know nothing. Ask him, if his life would depend on a surgery for example, would he give himself on the hand of a professional or a relative or friend;

4. Doesn't have the courage to decide alone
Find out who is the decision factor (mother, father, husband, wife, etc.) and invite that person along to a discussion. Explain that that person deserves to know, like him, professional information;

5. Tries to "dodge" you
These people either have no confidence in them but show the opposite, either aren't interested in your offer but are trying to hide it and want to put you in difficulty by devious questions showing that they are. Only experience will help you detecting them in time and stay away from them;

6. Throws out false objections
People will throw you false objections to hide their real problem, or to gain confidence. The art is to discover that

objection and to take it to pieces as to arrive at a positive solution for both the prospect and you. You can recognize false objections as they are made to sound "good". There are probably hundreds, but here are 21 of the most common examples:

- I have no money;
- I have no time;
- People don't have money;
- I'm not the kind of person to deal with it;
- I don't know enough people;
- I don't know people interested in that;
- Products are expensive;
- By now, everyone deals with it;
- The market is already full;
- What if the market is saturated?
- Only those who started a long time ago earn money;
- It sounds too good (to be true);
- To be successful you also need luck;
- I'm too young / too old for this;
- This business will not work here (in this country);
- Soon the Internet will change the state of this activity;
- X also did something like this but he gave up;
- I love my work (job) and I am satisfied, I don't want to change anything;
- I've been to a similar meeting and it didn't convince me;
- This is a pyramid scheme;
- The end of the world is coming soon anyway...

In trade literature there are several methods of getting and handling objections, of which I have chosen to show you a few that you can use quickly:

Conditional closure method - is a very effective method because through the objection's solution you will reach even closing the sale.
The technique is based on the principle of reciprocity - if I solve your problem, you will buy the product / start the collaboration instead.

For example: "You say that you aren't interested in nothing more than the blue product. If I call the store and you'll get a blue product, I understand that the problem is solved? "

The method of the three "F": Feel, Felt, Find solution
This method is based on handling the objection in three steps:

• First step - *Feel* - empathize with the client / prospect: "I understand what you feel about this product, it seems ..."

• Step Two - *Felt* - move focus to another person, creating objectivity: "Another customer / prospect also felt the same"

• Step Three – *Find solution* - force client's confidence by finding the solution: "Still after a day of use he liked the product very much and considered it indispensable.

Another method that I propose is a method called AILA (an acronym for the four steps you need to take). These steps are:

Amortization - the stage where you show empathy towards the client / prospect and you disperse tension. Phrases such as: "I understand your surprise ..." "I too was surprised, same as you" "Your point of view is correct", etc.

At this stage it is necessary to defuse tension. If you will attack the objection directly then you risk slipping in an exchange of words that don't lead to closing the sale.

Interrogating - is the stage where by formulating open questions you find out the problems that displease the client / prospect and you separate true objections from false objections. It is extremely important at this stage to properly treat real objections; handling false objections will carry you on a false trail and you will shift you away from the sale target. The right questions are: "Why do you think that?", "What else do you expect from this collaboration?", "How do you think we should do? etc.

Listening - is the stage where you stimulate the client / prospect to talk as much as possible about him and any problems he might have. It is absolutely natural to listen with interest the client's / prospect's responses to the previous questions. The appropriate gestures and words ("Yes ... I understand!") will make him explain in detail his desires so that you understand what goals he aims.

Answer - is the stage where you have to give an answer to client's / prospect's objection. This response is recommended to be as specific as possible and to the point, about his problem and formulated in the form of benefits he may receive. The answer will be formulated so as to close the objection and to help you close the sale, otherwise the client / prospect will raise a new objection. Regardless what the objection might be, make sure that this is the real reason for hesitating. For example: *I have no money;* Ask, apart from the fact that ... (eg you have no money) what else makes you hesitate?

"It's too expensive" - Answer: we propose you various options that can accommodate to your budget. Now that this is clear, how much are you willing to invest in your future?
(Negotiate other versions of business or products packages, explaining the difference in comfort / effort).

"The products are expensive"
What is that expensive? You know, we have nothing against those who sell cheap, as they know best how much what they offer is worthing;

"I have no money!"
You have no money now or in general? How do you see a solution to your problem?

• Ben Franklin Method: Why yes, why no*

In the left side of the table write the benefits that your prospect will get. After you play them out, lay the pen to the prospect and encourage him to write the disadvantages to the right, then let him examine for himself.

Why YES	Why NO
....	....
....	....
....	....
....	....

• The sheet - Method*

Take a sheet of paper and write on half of it the benefits and on the other half the price value of the products or business and tell your prospect "when our meeting ends, only two things can happen."

Tear the sheet in two and give him the half with the benefits saying: "I leave you the information containing the benefits that our collaboration brings and I keep the countervalue of the products"; then lay him the half containing the countervalue of the products and withdraw the benefits: "I remain with the business and all the products and their benefits and I leave you their countervalue."Which one do you choose??

Regardless of the outcome leave the client to go home with the sheet - he will be able to reflect on that.

• What is the problem? Method*

Write on a sheet of paper the problems that the prospect says he has, and next to them write the business or products price and ask, "Which of these two is the problem? As I understand price seems to be the problem, but the real problem is that you will be left outside with the problems that you already have, the products and business price is in fact the key for solving them! "
This technique can be used as a completion to the 'sheet' method.

Regardless of the outcome leave the client to go home with the sheet – he will be able to reflect on that.

"I have to think about it"
Make sure you guessed what it's behind this response. Usually this means: I want to know more, give me more details. Help me decide!

"What exactly you have to think about? Is it the price or if you are seriously interested to start a business?

WAIT for the answer!

If you fail to close the discussion favorably, ask:

- "Do you want me to explain you any specific point? Do you have more questions? You told me that you are seriously motivated to start your business! Let's think together! "

"I'm not interested"
I understand that you're not interested in your and your family's prosperity?
After this question you will usually reach an objection presented above.

"I don't trust your company, because I have never heard of it"
This is why we first met and I gave detailed information, I wanted you to know from the very beginning that when we talk about our company in our field is like saying you don't trust Microsoft in the computers. We have been on the market for X years, in X countries, with over X millions satisfied customers and distributors. And by the way, the most important is that people are really getting results with this business (you show and you talk about the results).

"I don't have time"

You want more time? If you work as you do now, will you have?

Surprising that you mention it! Our business has a smart way to multiply your time and money.

"I don't know people interested"
Don't you know anyone interested about health, beauty, extra income, etc?

Did you know that in Network Marketing the largest networks consist mainly of people who haven't known each other before?

"I do not want to hear about MLM"
I know what you're thinking, because I thought so too before I met a professional. But when I understood the many advantages offered by this activity, of course I think differently now. It is a booming industry that can help you work and live at a level that you determine.

The objection for a real seller / negotiator is a great opportunity to close the deal!

In conclusion to the objection subject, remember this important idea - If you do harm with these techniques, you will feel guilty and you will wake up after a period not truly enjoying what you got. Use this information only for the purpose of dealing with false objections and get to the real ones. Remember that your target is helping the real ones. Remember that your target is helping the prospect to make a positive decision for him first!

*Source: Bogdan Ficeac, Manipulation Techniques (Second Edition), Nemira Publishing House, 1997

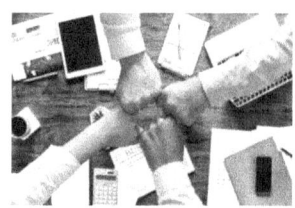

The key word for this type of business is "teamwork"! Therefore, there is the term of professional start (fast start) and the concept of "key man". The advice of those who are successful in this area is that since the moment you started and up to a level of stability, you shouldn't do anything by yourself.

All the issues covered so far (setting goals, making a list of names, invitation for discussion, business opportunity presentation, finalizing the discussion and starting a partnership) can be seen and used by any type of business. However, from this point going forward to the principles of teamwork, we move away from traditional businesses almost exclusively on the "playground" for building a multi-level network. Here, through training, observation of personal example, it will all duplicate into good or bad, with direct consequences for your new business partner and your own business.

Professional start means to accustom your new partner and to learn him how to correctly use the "system of training and guidance", to help him develop those habits and that way of thinking that in network-marketing industry make the difference between long term success and failure.

Professional start is designed to make your new partner understand the importance of these habits for himself and to apply them for his success. Let's see how to do a professional start of your new partner and which the steps that you should follow are in fact:

1. The Package of products

The professional start is recommended to begin with a detailed presentation for the package of products bought by the new person (to become a partner or customer of our company).
The presentation gives clear explanations on the benefits of these products, and also on how to use or manage them.
If you start a person, partner or customer, professionally, your network will be a healthy one and will have a proper basis for multiplying the business. If you're thinking to "sell" only the business plan, you will end up with people entering your network that will do exactly the same thing: they will place other businesses without consuming for themselves and without recommending others to consume. This way during the months in which they won't find new partners, the frustration caused by
the lack of turnovers will appear. A strong network will

contain as many consumers as possible and some good network builders, who themselves will do the same.

2. Finding and writing the goals

It is very important for the one who begins to know what he wants from him, from you and from the opportunity you two have initiated. Once the target is set, the ways to achieve it and the period of time must be identified.

3. Do the list name together

Start from a top 20 and after you finish the "start" call together a few people to invite them to a discussion or to a company or business guidance system event.

4. Ethics

Your obligation when you start out with a new person is to explain him in detail the role of ethics in this activity.

Ethics should be a permanent vector, first in your thinking, because then your actions will be the same. You have to think and behave in the way that you want to multiply in your organization. You have to warn the new partner that most probably he won't understand certain principles from the beginning, but if it doesn't agree with them and apply them in his business then he'll move with the handbrake on. Therefore if there is any question, he must always ask his advice line on any element which seems to be unclear. Success in network marketing often means giving up outside rules, the logic based on competition and on win-lost life philosophy. This activity is different from what he has learned and done so far and until he makes serious money, he will have to obey the instruction and guidance system in order to convince himself of its effectiveness.

And, as in any other business, here too are some unwritten rules that must be carefully followed, based on universal principles such as:

- "What you personally don't like, you shouldn't do to others", that is for example, if you meet someone who has already had a discussion with a parallel line about the opportunity within 48 hours, you shouldn't intrude, just praise the business and that person even if you don't know him personally;

- "Don't say what you don't want to hear," that is not bringing injuries ever;

- Manage money properly. Many times you will have to take cash in advance for tickets to various seminars, information materials or packages of products. These situations must be managed carefully, written and contracts kept in a folder dedicated to the activity.

5. Rights and obligations

From the very start you must settle the rights and obligations of each other. The new partner should be aware that conformation to his obligations is actually the key to success.

New person's right is to receive support from the mentoring line (professional start, 1:1 presentations with his guests in the first two weeks and also "finalisations" in the first month). Meanwhile, he has "an obligation" to train individually (reading recommended materials: books, audiobooks, etc.) and to participate in business events.

6. Attitude

In order to learn and to be effective it's necessary to have a small ego. Explain the new person that regardless of statute or education he might have in other areas, here he's at start and he should be a serious and disciplined student. If he learns the mechanism, he'll receive the extraordinary benefits of multiplication.

Therefore, his opened and positive attitude from the very beginning and then throughout the whole process of building the business will allow the new partner to take full advantage of the financial opportunity. Positive attitude in our business may be represented by:

• Positive thinking;

- Large-mindedness;
- Medium to long term perspective vision;
- Patience;
- Sense of humor;
- Acquiring new knowledge without reluctance;
- Facing social fears.

And let's never forget that attitude determines altitude!

7. Explain him the importance of the seven habits of a key person

You must make him understand that as quickly as he learns these habits, so he will be able to increase his business and to pass correctly and duplicable the relay to his future partners.

In network marketing, the one using correctly the "system of training and guidance" and following certain habits is called generically a "key person".

Interestingly, all successful distributors in the multi-level network industry are "key people".

These seven habits we are talking about are:

1. To be 100% consumer of products from your own business
(to be the product of your products. Leading by example is one of the main keys to success in MLM)

2. You present the business opportunity and the products to at least 15 people in a month;

3. You monthly bring minimum two new consumers
(it is easy to meet this criterion of the key person: for example, most people who don't want to do the business can become your clients);

4. You self-develop and read daily
(it is obvious that instead of watching the news or any other negative things at TV much profitable is to read business books or for self-development. Good books educate the spirit, develop your thinking, creativity and will improve your social relationships);

5. You train listening daily to related audio-books
(in the car, in traffic, in the morning or in the evening at home. Audio-books will help you to train, will give you focus and will be your support during the delicate moments. It is also a very handy way to increase your attitude);

6. Actively participate in meetings organized by the company or by the "system of training and guidance"
(the importance of participating at all events related to building your business goes on two things, perseverance and training, and both criteria can be met by using the events that will deliver every time fresh information and you'll keep you motivated.

On the other hand, you want your partners to multiply that. No need to tell you that if you attend the event, then your people will attend it too, will learn and will gain the right skills, they will find new motivations);

7. You are a team player (teamwork)
"Teamwork is the ability to work together in order to achieve a common idea, the ability to direct individual accomplishments towards organizational goals. It is the source that allows common people to attain uncommon results." Andrew Carnegie - the richest man in the world in 1901

In building network business, teamwork is a different concept than in traditional businesses in the sense that it's not only collaboration or opinion exchange, but it's an ethic and strong synergistic relationship built on predetermined principles without which you'll never become a "key person", but if respected, will make you an example to follow both in the business organization which you belong to and in everyday life.

These principles are:

1. ENLIGHTENING;
2. CONSULTING;
3. RESPECTING CROSSLINE;
4. DUPLICATE.

1. Enlightening

The concept of enlightening is to bring into light, to reveal something in an honest manner. Enlightening is a way to choose a behavior in which you decide to focus and to see the positive attributes and actions of an individual, organization or whatever, even if you're aware that there aren't only positive qualities.

In daily life we have the chance to meet this human basic need to feel important to someone.
Thus, we can compliment them and we can recognize certain efforts and their importance. We can tell people how are appreciated they are and we can congratulate them, honor them in many ways. There is a strong link between being good and having a quality life. One of the ways we can be good is to highlight what is good in others and praise sincerely.

Specific to our business, by enlighening we can build a good and accurate picture of all the elements of the business: training and guidance system, seminars, guidance line, downline partners and parallel lines partneres, working tools (books, CDs, DVDs) and of course, products.

Enlightening will not be in any way a free eulogy, it will actually be a legitimate transfer that you have in front of your prospect to all elements of your work in building the business.

• The business is enlightened primarily through punctuality at meetings and seminars, through discipline and through a professional attitude. Also, you enlighten your business by training on all aspects related to the work you do: economic performance of the company, technology and product innovation, guidance system of the business, etc.

• Enlightening the events is speaking openly and positively about the speakers, about the information that will be offered and about the usefulness of the presence there.

• Interpersonal enlightening (eg the presentation you make to your guiding line or your partners) can be thought as a good football game ball, followed by backward pass to teammate (when you present the prospect to your guiding line, enlightening your mentor and he returns your enlightening, giving the prospect confidence in you). Therefore it's desirable to work in the same place (business location, work centre or coffee house) with your guidance line, with the parallel lines and downlines. It's the only way you'll be able to get legitimacy in front of your prospects (or else you should praise yourself, which is neither ethical nor productive);

As shown above, enlightening is done both by words and by actions. For example, if you're just starting out and you work with your guidance line, it goes without saying that when you're in a conversation with a prospect, you will not text messages, you will not leave the table to talk on the phone and you will not correct him in the presentation, even if you think he forgot to say something. If you will do these things you have have enlightened with words in vain if you make the contrary by facts.

It is proven that those using enlightening the best are also becoming excellent team players and quickly attract success.

2. Consulting
"Always there will be two: a master and a disciple" – Yoda

Consultation is met in one way or another in many types of businesses. The entrepreneur is often the man who thinks he knows and can do everything. But looking at only from the personal perspective, things can be seen a little bit distorted and you'd better always listen an objective point of view coming
from outside.

The ideas, enthusiasm and courage are necessary but not sufficient conditions for having a successful business.

Unlike the other types of businesses of any kind, in our industry consultation is usually provided free of charge by someone in the guidance line, because he has more experience, is objective (looking from outside at your business) and is co-interested in your success. The role of the consultation is to help you grow your business in an efficient and professional manner.

As a clever network builder, you will consult only with those in your guidance line for the simple reason that relatives, friends and your aquaintances, even if they want to support you through their advice, are simply not good at. If they want to help you, they will trust you and will give you moral support. You will not consult with any other network builders either, as it is obvious that they have no direct interest for your business whatsoever.

Consultation should not be confused with asking for advice for or in special situations. It represents setting meetings for the beginning of the calendar month (when planning is made together with the guidance line) and the progress is discussed ten days before the end of the working month. Besides consultation with your guidance line, you will offer consultation to your downlines also, giving them your experience. We can compare consultation with a football coach work, who at the beginning of the game has a strategy and puts it into practice with the team and who during the match re-examines it and re-checks it, making any necessary adjustments in order to win the game. Consultation is benefical and very important for the health of your business and must be multiplied in your downlines. Beware though, the basic idea is that first you have to be trainable and then to be willing to train others.

As a principle of communication, the negative things are transmitted only up and down only the positive things go. The guidance line must know the problems (if any) and together find solutions, while downline should be morally encouraged and supported. Consultation is like vitamin for health, should be used for prevention and not just when there is an issue.

Rules and conclusions:

• Consultation is required from the guiding lines at the beginning and towards the end of a calendar month;

• Consultation is offered by the guidance lines that are not required to provide it, but agree this;

• Consultation will make good information flow to circulate for growing, without having negative things contaminating the network;

• Make so these principles are duplicated also by your partners in order to build and maintain a healthy business.

3. Crossline

The term crossline in network marketing means crossing business parallel lines that have no direct material interests from one another and is often compared to gossip. It is normal to respect and to communicate with people you've met and you meet all the time on various events organized by the guidance and training system of the company and have extraordinary human relationships, but under no circumstance you should ask for advice about the business and also should not listen to such advice. It is understood that the parallel line is not interested in your success in building the business. In the history of network-marketing, huge networks were poisoned and collapsed due to negative crossline.

However, crossline situations may be:

• Positive - when for example, parallel lines work together at an event for scheduling and organizing the room, the conference, etc.

• Neutral - when parallel lines do not discuss anything related to building the network;

• Negative - when vital signs of the personal business or parallel line's business are discussed (results, number of guests, the estimated turnovers, etc).

It is necessary to avoid negative crossline situations because your network builder business starts, operates, maintains and grows, including by the fact that you have a positive attitude towards this opportunity, the company you work with and the training and guidance system, and every untrue or negative information may become destructive for your attitude. This scattered and spread to your downlines can be associated with a virus that infects your entire network structure.

Here is the crossline situation:

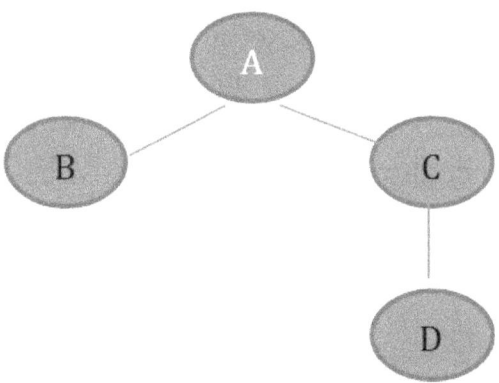

We agree that A, B, C, D are four people in a multi-level network organization and are all working with the same company.
Here (A) is the guiding line for (B), (C) and (D). (A) is interested in the success of all (B, C, D) downlines.

At his turn, (C) is guidance line for (D) and is directly interested in the success of this person.

(B) is in crossline position with (C) and vice versa, the same for (B) and (D).
Specifically:

• positive information flows down from (A) to (B), from (A) to (C), from (C) to (D) and from (A) to (D);

• positive information goes up from (B) to (A), from (C) to (A), from (D) to (C), from (D) to (A);

As you can see, even if it's positive information, it should not be transmitted from (B) to (C) and vice versa or from (D) to (B) and vice versa, in order not to turn into negative crossline.

• negative information always goes up only from (B) to (A), from (C) to (A), from (D) to (C) and from (D) to (A).

• negative information will never go from (A) to (B), from (A) to (C) or (D) or from (C) to (D), being considered negative crossline.

Pay attention, negative crossline is made not only by the one who improperly sends the information, but also by the one who actively or passively receives it.
If we make a similitude again with a football game, the phenomenon of negative crossline is such as the players wouldn't listen to the tactical advice of the coach, but to the spectators in the stands or even worse, to the opponent on the ground.

4. Multiplication / duplication
Right from the beginning, it is imperative for you to understand that between a classic business and a network-marketing one, the most important difference is multiplication.

If in the first case, in most situations, you only earn from what you personally accomplish or by paying employees, in the second case you will get income also from those who "adhere" to your organization as independent businesses. This means that your main activity is looking for partners and transmitting them your experience and your upperline's. According to this principle you must make sure that your downlines are copying you at their turn.

Network marketing allows you to get tremendous financial incomes only through multiplication: in working with the team as a whole, the energy and the accomplishments of the group will duplicate and that's the only way you'll build a solid business.

Therefore, you must be careful so things are done right to the end; network-marketing professionals warn us that EVERYTHING MULTIPLIES. All seen, but mostly what is not seen, both good things and the bad ones.

For this, every step you make in this business has to answer affimatively to the following questions: Do I want to replicate this in my business? Would I like my partners to do exactly what I do? Would it be useful to me? Be aware and attentive regarding the force of multiplication and be responsible towards your partners, because your goal is to multiply only good things in their business also. There is even a saying to this effect: it does not matter what works for me, it only matters what can be applied widely throughout my organization, what is multiplicable. That is why in order to have success in this business it takes perseverance and just simple things, precisely for everyone to be able to learn and do.

Practically, in your daily activities, duplication looks like this: if you have a notebook with written goals, if you do meetings, if you train yourself, if you attend the events, most of your partners will do the same. All will duplicate, the attitude that you have towards your guidance line and your inter-personal relationships but also negative crossline or the fact that you don't consult, for example.

To become and to be a "key person" – conclusion

To be or not to be a key person is as easy. But you can't be a key person unless you follow the recipe 100%. You can't negotiate the price. In order to use and cherish the above seven habits it takes a decision and not talent. Anyone can have other positive habits, but obeing these seven listed and described principles guarantees vastly your success in network-marketing industry, and perhaps in other areas of your life. It is, if you want, a process acquired and practiced with great discipline by an athlete. That will model you a winning attitude and will take you to success.

To build your network in a professional way, you have tools and support events which are not mandatory but without which it is unlikely to have a big business. You have to think at these tools and events like if they were some disciplined and efficient employees that help and ease your work enormously.

Working tools:

1. From the company

• Web page;
• Agreement on paper;
 • Company magazine;
 • Presentation brochures;
 • Info DVD;

2. From the bookstore

• Notebook size A4 wire-wove paper;
• Time table for scheduling meetings;
• Journals;

3. From the training and guidance system

• Presentation catalogue;
• Info DVDs;
• Audio-books about the steps of network builders;
• Recommended programme for monthly training / personal development (books and audiobooks);
• Journals;
• Books about network-marketing business concept;
• Tickets for zonal, regional, national and international conferences or technical seminars (workshops).

Events (conferences, technical seminars):

These are made to give information to prospects but also to maintain the motivation for those who are active in this area. As destination, events actually show who we represent, who we are, what we do and where we are going. Events in the field of network-marketing industry are organized either by the company or by the guidance and training system, as it follows:

1. Organized by the company:

• Most MLM large companies organize regional events on large areas (North America, Latin America, Asia, Europe, South Pacific, Africa) where products, technologies are being launched, market strategies are announced and business performers in the area are rewarded at open stage;

• Small circle information and consultation seminars with distributors who make the majors turnovers in the area in order to determine the strategy for the local market;

2. Organized by the training and guidance system:

• Open events (open) - these provide information about the business opportunity and in some measure products are being promoted. These conferences are usually weekly, at city / small region level;

• Regional or national conferences - here for several hours detailed information about the business is presented but also these events offer vision, how you can reach success. During these events are recognized and rewarded, at open stage, the performers in that region or country;

• International motivational and inspirational seminars - these are designed to dissect in detail everything related to business and the steps needed to be taken in order to be successful in this field. Are focusing specifically on providing vision, the conferences are designed to motivate and inspire both prospects and active people;

PART III TOOLS

PART III
TOOLS FOR MAKING THE DREAMS COME TRUE

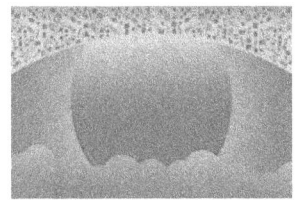

TIME MANAGEMENT

Time is a limited resource that can't be saved ... can only be spent ... in an EFFECTIVE way

It is a universal truth nowadays that we all need more time: to complete a project, to spend quality time with family and friends, to carry out the targets from your personal agenda or to start, put up and grow a business. When it comes to time, we realize that it's a limited resource whose management is very often left aside. Today there are many time management courses "in the market", but with a few principles we can effectively manage our life on our own.

Time management is much more than the ability to plan and manage time. Time management definition reads: it is a range of tools and approaches, their use leading to a more balanced and pleasant life and a more efficient usage of time.

Set your goals first and then the tasks
Proper management of time should begin with the goals you want to achieve, this way you'll know what you want and where you're going. The next move will be to define your tasks and goals in phases that must be overcome step by step, in order to achieve the ultimate goal;

The goal is not the activity, but the result itself
For example, if you decide to move to another country in two years and start a business there, one of your possible tasks would be learning the language of that country. Your goal is not an activity (learning the language), but the result of your activity (you will learn that language at an advanced level).

Another individual goal would be buying a course book - you have to go to the bookstore or call a foreign language course school. Likewise, you can achieve each goal by setting individual targets using a similar scheme. If you achieve individual goals, you can achieve faster your main target. The target is not the desire to work or setting too high expectations, but a simpler perception of the big picture regarding the way you personally have chosen to follow.

Are you a good planner?

The basis for planning is to understand the limits, the needs and spending sufficient time for preparation. There should be a rule at the end of each week to go over the list of priorities for the coming week and even for each day that follows.

It's great if you have a specific place for notes or lists of priorities. You should think about the planning breaks as a relaxing part of the day or as a compensation for the lost time. You really need to know the approximate time for tasks in order to correctly plan. Try to be realistic because a wrong schedule can lead to collapse. Therefore, it is easy to plan tasks at intervals of 30 minutes. If you have completed the task earlier, you can relax or you can work on less important tasks.

Do you wake up early in the morning or are you a night owl?

You should take into account your performance curve. There are people who like to work especially in the morning (the ones who get up early) and in the afternoon their activity is reduced. Others begin to be effective in the afternoon, and their work is more intense late at night (night owl).

It is good to know which is your physical utmost and when do you have a maximum alertness and concentration level and to plan your activities so - important and creative tasks. Plan your routine or administration work in times of low efficiency.

Four tipes of priorities
You say you have no time? You're actually saying that you do more important things!

Setting priorities will help you differentiate each task according to its importance. I divided the tasks into four groups:

• *Important and urgent* - tasks with deadlines, meetings, crisis situations, some phone calls and e-mails;

• *Important but not urgent* - less important meetings, some phone calls, difficult tasks but not trivial;

• *Unimportant but urgent* - interruptions due to other people's problems or minor requests of those around you;

• *Not important and not urgent* - web browsing, checking the email ten times, watching TV, etc.

Or in other words :
• Important + Urgent = do it now!
• Important + Not urgent= plan them!
• Unimportant + urgent= keep them!
• Unimportant + not urgent= give up on them!

Summarizing :

You get to cherish the time more when you don't have it. I don't advise you to become a workaholic, but neither some lazy person that don't realize that every lost second is not coming back!

Loss of time and how to escape it

The activities carried out without thinking that don't bring any benefit are called time-consuming activities:

- Each interruption of the activity;
- Long pauses;
- Daydreaming;
- Indirect search on the Internet;
- Chatting with colleagues;
- Starting work without useful information available;
- Allowing unnecessary tasks to overwhelm you;
- Postponement;
- Searching for documents due to the inadequate organization or unorganized workspace.

Peace and concentration

An important feature of efficiency is peace and concentration. Interruption causes distracting attention and reduces the ability to return to work. The more disturbed you are, the harder it will be to get back to work.

Practical advice

Keep track if you don't intentionally seek another activity that postpones your task.

If you start a new task, you should first consider the procedure. If you feel pressured and you aren't sufficiently focused, plan a personal session and concentrate on important activities.

Keep pen and notebook handy for notes and phone numbers. Establish deadlines for each task. If you impose deadlines, try to realize them sooner than you had planned. Avoid delays - this leads to a vicious circle. If you have whom to delegate, then delegate.

Remember that you can't please everybody. You can't carry out all tasks. It is essential to say "NO" and to be decided when it concerns your time and to respect other people's time.

How to start?

Change your attitude and learn new habits. Identify your strengths and weaknesses and respect them - exploit your strengths and work on weaknesses.

• Enclose individual goals in planning your time;
• Make a weekly plan and then a daily one;
• Make some time to plan and think these tasks;
• Organize your workspace;
• Analyze your habits and improve them.

Time management rules are not meant to be annoying, but should be welcome in managing your time, which will lead you to a more satisfying life and a less stressful working environment.

Understand your needs and don't be too strict with yourself. If you don't feel good and you know that your performance is not the very best, adjust your work and arm yourselve with new strengths.

Goals give the direction of your path, but don't forget the way itself because of the goals! Think about time management as a skill to control the events in your life. And the magic formula is in your hand!

Stephen R. Covey, Seven Habits of Highly Effective People or Wisdom Alphabet
All Publishing House, 2009
Source: http://www.grafton.ro/en/career-zone/time-management/

"It's easy to believe in yourself and to be disciplined when you're a winner, when you're number 1. But you need a lot more confidence and discipline until you're not yet a winner. "- Vince Lombardi

Discipline means to know and to write your ultimate goal, then to make a plan to follow immediately. What do you do today for your dream, what will you do this week, this month, this year? Make somehow so each step takes you closer. Briefly, you make a plan and you stick with it to the end, regardless of difficult times and challenges that might arise along the way.

In the beginning most certainly discipline is gonna seem like a limitation of freedom, because you'll have to do things that you don't like and because of that your body and mind will fight the change. But, precisely this process of change will bring you the freedom to get where you want to be and especially to define the person you will become in order to achieve this goal.

So, without a plan to follow orderly, your brain won't know what to do and where to take you, so it will go with the herd. Depending on what programs you watch TV and what kind of people you surround yourself with, it will react and guide you as such.

What will a discipline plan contain (thought, written and followed):

Internal motivation:
That's what motivates you and comes from inside you. Find the correct answer to the questions "Why is this dream important to me?" "What kind of person must I become in order to achieve this dream?"

Self-efficiancy:
In psychology, self-efficiancy means your expectations to successfully accomplish a goal with the resources and abilities today. If your self- efficiancy is high, then you'll be motivated to always get to action and you'll experience positive emotions on the steps that you go through. If you don't see yourself as capable, you'll delay and fight change and thus stand against achieving your goals.

Before you put up a strategy for your goal, think of at least five achievements that you've had throughout life. This way you'll set your mind to think about your resources and abilities and you'll look at yourself like being able to get over challenges. On the other hand, look for examples of other people who have succeeded in what you want to succeed. Identify what helped them and if you can, ask them what they have done in that regard.

Trust:
And here I mean both your confidence in yourself and in your goal. Imagine how you want to be in the future. Who will you be when you will achieve the goal? How will you feel? What will you see and what people you will have around?

Self-control:
In your strategy with the weekly and monthly activities also include key moments for when you are tempted to give in and give up.

Think about how you will handle the times when you are upset or you'll have no mood to go to work.

For example, choose and write a few sentences that you know motivate you, listen to a song you like or listen to a song you like or listen to an audiobook with a theme that inspires you. Then, it is useful to find a symbol for your goal. For example, if you want to be a good public speaker, you can think of a room full of people who listen to you. Take a picture with a full room, which looks like your mental image. Whatever you think helps works, so be creative.

Self-control is the most important step and you should never think that you're not a free man because you force yourself to stick to your plan.

Better think otherwise: if you give in too frequent to hang

outs with friends, if you will lazy sit at TV or the internet and you will postpone what is important to your life, you'll never be a free man. You will be a slave to night outs, to TV and internet, or to friends who pull you to go out only for a word, only today. Freedom actually means doing everything you utmost with the tools you have available for becoming the man you want to be!

Keep a journal:
Don't fall into the trap of thinking that your mind is a huge computer and you don't need notes. You should know that once you've put a plan on paper, your brain immediately seeks ways and resources to motivate you and push you to action, and more than that, it will push you to results. A whispered or even loudly said goal will keep you motivated for a few days. A written and planned step by step goal will place you on the road to success. Can you choose?

In the journal you will write both your progresses and challenges that you've met along the week, what came to your mind when you hit a snag and what methods you can keep and add to your plan to improve it.

And don't forget to check whenever you have achieved something. No matter how small the step taken forward is, it will motivate you to see that you stick to the plan.

Yet it is important to be flexible too. That means seeing what works for you and what doesn't and to do the necessary adjustments throughout the plan. Focus on the improvements that you can do today in order for the plan to work better tomorrow.

Learn new things
Do your best to talk with people who can help you with valuable information, read and go to seminars. You'll find that those who succeded didn't have any luck, skills or any special talents, and that behind their success are actually a lot of hours of work, struggle with themselves and discipline. Develop the skills you need to achieve your plan. In short, learn new things from people who have succeeded and apply them in your life.
When you hear others saying about you that you were lucky, it means that you can look back and realize that you have developed healthy habits, you have self-educated, you did even things you didn't like, and now you get to do exactly what you like, and when you look at who you've become ... you're the person you wanted to be.

Source: http://entuziasm.ro/dezvoltare-personala/
sase-etape-pentru-un-plan-de-disciplina/

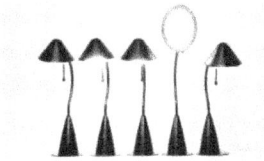

Attitude is the way you see the world. "Two men look out through the bars of a prison. One sees mud, the other sees the stars." What do you see?

What is attitude?
Attitude is a mental positioning towards a mindset or an experience, or a person
al orientation towards your faith. A positive attitude is therefore the general tendency to be optimistic and confident in achieving your hopes.

Attitude may be:
• Feeling;
• Perspective;
• Point of view;
• Conception.

We have all heard numberless statements about how important the attitude we have in everyday life is. The link between attitude and success is indisputable. Meanwhile, the change in attitude may be one of the hardest things we can do, says John Maxwell, one of the most influential leaders worldwide.

He also states that the right attitude is not enough to get what you want. "I know a lot of people who have a great attitude, but still they have not fulfilled their dreams. Attitude is not everything, but it is the main thing that makes the difference. "

In a simplistic approach, attitude can be compared to a mental filter through which a man can see the world:

Negative filter - the empty half of the glass:

A man with a negative attitude is characterized by the phrase "I can't"

• Insists on problems;
• Find defects in everything;
• Sees the limits.

Optimistic filter - the full half of the glass:

A man with a positive attitude can be characterized by the phrase "I can"

• Focuses on solutions;
• Searches for the positive aspects;
• Sees the opportunities.

The effects of a positive attitude:

Negative attitude creates you false limits and destroy your

energy reserves. It can eliminate future opportunities and limit any evolution. In contrast, positive attitude is focused on building and fixing. When you adopt it, you'll be able using language and gestures to motivate others around you and help them even when they don't know how to help themselves.

With a positive attitude in life, you can create deeper connections with people in your community or with your business partners and you will have access to many roads to success.

Encouraging compassion and creativity, you will spread positive energy around, which could be used by others to also think positively and in time you will create a domino effect.

Analyze your interactions with others and see how much you rely on reproaches and tough criticism and how much on solutions and suggestions for improvement. If you have more negative interactions than positive, it is time to change something in your life with positive thinking.

Positive attitude will help you:
• get easier over the problems and negative experiences; with positive thinking you can recover more quickly after a disappointment;
• highlight your accomplishments and successes and not still analyzing failures;
• become a model for others, from which others feel they

have something to learn;
• collaborate easier with those in your community and your partners and to get their support quicker when you'll have an initiative;
• better argue on your behalf, but also on behalf of others, which opens up even more many possibilities for you;
• have a greater influence on people;
• build your reputation as a person who deserves trust and respect;
• empower those that you interact with to adopt a positive attitude;
• find easier ways to achieve success that does not involve failure for the competition.

Even if the environment you live in or work in is mostly negative, changing the way of thinking can be a key element to your personal and professional success, which can lead in time even to environment change.

Only when you analyze your interactions with others and discover a report 5/1 (five positive interactions to one negative) you can truly say that you really have a positive attitude that helps you change your life in better.

Source: Jeff Keller, Attitude is everything, Curtea Veche Publishing House, 2005
http://www.nlpmania.ro

I am sure that at least once in life it has happened to each of us to realize that what we say is not important, but the way we say it. This is why some people will be more convincing than others, even if they are pronouncing the same words.

Research revealed that in interpersonal communication, 55% of the message you communicate is delivered through body language - non-verbal element (gestures and attitude), 38% is transmitted through paraverbal elements (tone, pace and voice volume) and only 7% is given through words (verbal element itself).

It's like thoughts and feelings are actually "written on the forehead," printed in gestures, attitude and supported by posture. The good news is that you can use all this in your favor. On one hand, you can better control your body language and tone to express exactly what you want to communicate while on the other hand, paying more attention to others' body language, you'll be able to know them better and communicate more efficiently with them.

Body language contributes to communication by facial expression, body movement (gestures), posture, general appearance and tactile communication.

1. Facial expression: mimicry, smile and look

Mimicry:
• contracted forehead- concern, anger, frustration;
• raised eyebrows, open eyes - wonder, surprise;
• tight-drown lips - uncertainty, hesitation, hiding information.

Smile:
Is a very complex gesture that can express a wide range of information, from pleasure, joy, satisfaction to promise, cynicism or embarrassement.

Laughter:
Is an exclusive expression for mankind, representing the limited response of a unique behavior that reflects inner feelings. Laughter releases inner tensions.
Acoustic analysis of laughter indicated that it may contain one of the following vowels:

A - such laughter sounds open, liberating and heartfelt; is typical for people who don't deceive others;

E - this laughter sounds nasty, like a bleat; is the expression of a lack of respect, has evil and contempt connotations;

I - this laughter is observed at young people or the ones who want to look younger; this kind of laughter is also known as "laughing inside"; is usually an ironic laugh;

O - this kind of laugh corresponds to tensionate or surprise reactions; this way of laughing means a defense reaction of somebody to whom most probably something unpleasant happened; depending on the intensity of the sound, it can express: anger, protest or even hate;

U - so laughs a person who is gripped by terror; this laughter indicates rejection of a person, an object or an experience or keeping them away.

Look:
How we look and we are looked at is related to our needs for approval, acceptance, trust and friendship. To look or not to look at someone always has a meaning. Looking at someone confirms that we recognize his presence, the fact that he exists for us; intercepting someone's look reflects the desire to communicate. A direct look can mean honesty, intimacy, but in certain situations, can communicate threat. In general, an insistent and continous look will bother.

Making short intermittent eye contact indicates no friendship. Looking sideways or not looking at someone can show lack of interest, distance. Avoiding the look means hiding feelings, discomfort or guilt.

Dilated Pupils show strong emotions. Pupils widen, generally, at a pleasant sight or when we have a sincere attitude. Pupils contract as an expression of displeasure. Frequent blinking indicates anxiety.

Face is the most expressive part of the body. Specialists in the field divided human faces into six major types:

• Square type - is considered to be energetic, active, with the will to achieve, authoritative, vain;

• Rectangular - needs activity and dominance, but is the most theoretic one and shows less force in achieving the objectives;

• Long face - hypersensitive, pessimistic, meditation;

• Triangular - is cerebral, daring, original, adventurous, imaginative, and unstable;

• Round type - has a warm temper, aerial, sanguineous, cheerful, optimistic, with passenger sorrows;

• Oval - is full of charm, has artistic inclinations and a diplomatic character, is rather passive and has a low physical strength.

Body moves:

In the professional literature were established seven main

groups of facial expressions, although each group has many variations. These are: happiness, surprise, fear, sadness, anger, curiosity and disgust / contempt. These groups of facial expressions seem to be recognized signals in all human societies; therefore it is believed that there may be natural. We can say that each part of our face communicates: contracted forehead signifies concern, anger, frustration; wrinkled nose - discomfort and smile - means a confirmation of the availability for dialogue.

Regarding the eye contact with the interlocutor or his look, it's about how the look is fixed upon the other. About 80% of the time in a conversation our eyes are walking on the face of the one we are talking with. Avoiding this contact is a sign of shyness or guilt, anxiety.

In an official meeting, keeping the look in a triangle between the two eyes and the center of the forehead sends the message of seriousness and interest. In a friendly meeting, the look defines a triangle between the eyes and mouth. In all scenarios, keeping eye contact is important. If this contact fluctuates, the message is deficient. Keeping eye contact means continuous contact for thirty seconds.

The look oriented rather up reveals that that man is in a mental process of visualization. Horizontal look shows experiencing a mental process of hearing, and looking down reveals concern about one's own inner state.

For over ninety percent of the right-handed slipping into the past of the mind is accompanied by eye movement to the left, and imagining future plans makes the eyes go right. Therefore, without being sure, when the person we are talking with tells us how much he had worked the night before, until late at night in order to complete his tasks, but his eyes keep slipping to right up, you have the chance to listen to a false version of what actually happened.

Tactile communication is manifested by the frequency of the touch, by the way to shake hands, the way to hug, etc. Most of these gestures show closeness between people, familiarity.

Arms and hands are the "tools" in negotiations. In rest position, at the person standing, they are naturally hanging freely down. When sitting on a chair, arms and hands will sit relaxed in your lap or on the arms of the chair.

The hand is most commonly used in body language. Hand contact is the peak of preparations for opening a discussion / negotiation. This way data about your condition in that moment is transmitted. If you give a soft, flabby hand, there is no need to wonder if the person to whom you layed the hand will consider you soft and powerless. Nor shaking the hand with power leaves a pleasant impression.

The British and the Germans eventually shake hands at the arrival and take-off from the negotiation, however, the French, Russians, Italians and Spanish shake hands with the same person several times a day. If in France people shake hands regardless of sex, in England this gesture is met more in men and less in women or between a man and a woman.

With different people we shake hands differently. Hand contact, along with other signals, is a valuable indicator of the personality.

Rigid or authoritative people often force involuntary the interlocutor's hand to turn face up. On the other hand, those who reach out the hand palm up have a defensive nature, being always ready to surrender. The aggressive ones, especially those who cover their insecurity this way, are using hand like a nip. Avoiding involvement in relation is shown by the fast withdrawal of the hand. What is recommended? Hold the full palm and also let your hand to be held by the other's hand. Contact needs to be firm without being harsh, and detachment of the hands must be in the same time with your partner. Usually a handshake lasts three seconds.

Putting hands in your pockets usually means hiding insecurity or shows disinterest for discussion or negotiation and in formal discussions is perceived as a lack of courtesy.

Touching the face with the hand attracts the attention and tells that the person is lying or trying to lie. Of course, this should be interpreted according to the context.

Most moves of those who lie are: touching the chin, covering the mouth, touching the nose, rubbing the cheeks, caressing the hair, pulling the earlobe.

Carrying the hand to mouth is an expression of the tendency to control ourselves. Unconsciously something must be hiden or face mimicry must be hidden, the information being this way censored and the words blocked.

Head resting in palm shows boredom; but hand (with fingers) on the cheek, shows a lot of interest.

When people feel stressed or threatened, frightened, often feel the desire to have something in the mouth, and the most common forms of calming are smoking and chewing gum. Smokers often use cigarettes to calm and to control nervousness.

Posture (body position):

Communicates primarily social status that people have or want to have. A dominant person tends to keep his head hading up and a person with a humble attitude hanging down. In general, bending over the body shows interest towards the one you're talking with, but sometimes also anxiety, concern. A relaxed position, leaning in the chair on the back, may indicate detachment, boredom or faith in yourself but also a defense signal for those who feel they have a superior status comparing with the one they are communicating with.

Types of postures:

• of inclusion – or not inclusion: the posture that limits access within a group. For example, the members of a group may form a circle, may turn to the center, to stretch an arm or a leg over the interspace remained free, showing by all this that the access to this group is limited;

• of body orientation - refers to the fact that two people can choose to sit one in front of the other or side by side. The first position shows a predisposition for conversation, and the second - neutrality.

• of congruence - incongruence – the posture that communicates the intensity with which a person is involved in what the interlocutor says or does. Intense participation leads to congruent posture (similar to the partner's); change of the other's posture triggers in this case the change of the posture for the one heavily involved in communication. Where status, view or opinion differences exist between communicators, the incongruent positions appear: the person doesn't look to his partner and doesn't interact in any way.

Chest crossover of the arms shows the withdrawal inside. Since this gesture symbolizes a certain inability to defend, it also symbolizes a degree of subordination to the one in issue, express the willingness to defend. For some people this gesture is part of submissive gestures or expressing reverence for someone.

With the arms and hands close to the sides soldiers in the army sit. It is a posture that denotes submission and obedience but not simply obedience, but obedicence in this situation towards a boss or a higher degree.

The person who keeps his legs straight when sitting on a chair feels safe. The one who stands with his feet far-off is showing indifference. The farer the legs, the greater the indifference, lack of discipline, sometimes lack of education.

When someone sits cross-legged between two other persons you will found that the knee of the covered leg is oriented towards the person perceived as nicer.

Hand in the hip, elbow pulled out, has the role to amplify the power we shed. In the same time the hands on hips are no longer able to be used. This attitude is shown by arrogant people, in order to produce the impression of dominance. When hands and arms are kept under the table that person is not prepared to deal with the given situation and is afraid to show his hands, to take part in discussion, or believes that the hands will betray his insecurity, excitement and nervousness. If the hands are on the table, it reflects the ability and desire to establish contact.

The behavior of a person in a discussion judging from the movement of the body can be:

•characterized by lateral moves, they are considered to be good communicators;
• characterized by moves front-back – they are considered to be men of action;
• characterized by vertical movements, they are considered persuasive men.

2. Personal presence - communicate through body shape, clothing, smell, jewelry and other fashion accessories

Tall people are often employed in jobs that involve direct contact with customers, because of the respect that sometimes height attracts. Studies show that people with a pleasing appearance are considered more credible than those with less charm.

"Artefacts" means clothing, jewelery, perfumes, cosmetics, etc. They are used as an extension of the person wearing them, so in order to create an image of that person. Clothes can be used to create a role in negotiation situations. Clothing and accessories can state real or alleged social status. For example, women who accede to a high managerial position will usually tend to dress in a particular way (sober two-piece suit), wearing accessories similar to men (eg briefcase). For business situations stylish and quality but not sophisticated clothing is appreacited.

Clothing, as an extent of a personal choice, reflects the individual's personality, is kind of an extension of self, and in this context, communicates information about it. For example, if you have a nonconformist fashion style, this wants to communicate that you consider yourself original, maybe a social rebel or artist. Bright colors are chosen by action, communicative, outgoing people, and the pale ones by shy, introverted persons.

For a negotiator or a businessman, knowing the rules of nonverbal communication is essential because it represents more than half of direct communication. However, to avoid misinterpretation of an element in body language is good to interpret it in the context of all other verbal and nonverbal elements. Individual personality characteristics, education, life experience, etc., are factors to be considered in the correct interpretation of nonverbal language.

Source: Allan Pease, Body Language. How to read others' thoughts by their gestures, Polimark Publishing House, 1997 | Allan&Barbara Pease, Communication Skills, Curtea Veche Publishing House, 2007 | Collet Peter, The Book of Tells. How can we read peoples' thoughts from their actions, Trei Publishing House, Bucharest, 2003 | Cucos C., Psychopedagogy, Polirom Publishing House, 1998 | Dinu M., Communication, Algos Publishing House, 2000 |
Leroy G., Dialogue in education, Polirom Publishing House, 1998 | Paun E., School Sociopedagogy, Educational & Pedagogic Publishing House, 1982 | Soitu L., Communication pedagogy, Educational & Pedagogic Publishing House
http://www.ziaronline.eu/2011/06/06/limbajul-nonverbal-in-negociere

„The effort is showing fruits after a person refuses to stop"- Napoleon Hill

Perseverance is that feature that gives you strength of character. Usually perseverent people are powerful, with high emotional intelligence and who know how to channel their inner strength in order to carry out what they have started. At the opposite pole are those weak people who give up easily their goals because of despair, or inpatience or delay in having an outcome fastly.

Perseverance is powered by a long-term motivation supported by the image of a faraway goal. The motivation behind the perseverance is qualitative and burns like a dull flame, always ready to give a boost when obstacles arise. Goal or destination are always the main driver of this motivation, and as long the last one exists, there will also be perseverance.

A man's perseverance is tested in several steps:

Enthusiasm
The stronger that starting boom is, the faster the

motivation can be extinguished which compared, at halfway, will not seem as strong as it was in the beginning.

Unforeseen obstacles
In order to meet a goal, we are mentally prepared to face certain obstacles. But how things nature makes the unexpected appear all the time, there will be some moments that will dish what we originally planned. Many give up at this point.

Perseverance is more necessary than ever;

Other people's doubt
Understanding your goal up to a certain level, others won'tt give it the same value as you and that's why they will give up before you, having no reason to invest the motivation that you show. You will hear words like "can't you see it's not working, why don't you let it go?" Or "I don't think you'll succeed, I see you've been struggling for a long time and still you didn't make head or tail of it";

Own doubt
It won't be long until your doubt starts following others' doubts. Now you look for solutions, not with the same curiosity as in the beginning, but with an air of despair asking, "Are there any solutions left? ";

Deadlock
It is the stand-by moment. When you stop and you can't find a way anymore, a solution, a possibility. It's when

you're angry for your perseverance, you're angry that you'll never know if what you have proposed would work. All it remains is a question mark;

Sign from heaven

Metaphorically speaking, this stage is the one which gives the greatest satisfaction, the one that rewards perseverance in a magical way. The best solutions come unsought. A person talking about a totally different subject can give you an idea. Or a certain image can inspire you, without waiting that from it. Many artists and scientists have found solutions to their problems when they turned their back away to kneading and have taken a moment of respite. I too happened to distress on certain problems, and in the morning I simply woke up with solutions in mind. It's amazing how the brain works subconsciously, even when we sleep;

Reaching the goal

Whether it works or not, you've reached the point where you wanted to get. Certainty is on your side, whatever the outcome. The main satisfaction is that you removed all doubt and the feeling of surrender quits haunting. This point is perseverance's victory itself.

Do not give up!

Around the world, over time, there were people who really believed in what they wanted to do with their lives and dreams. So I'll offer some of the best known examples of personalities who have left something behind, even though they had moments when no one believed in them:

• The painter Van Gogh sold only one painting during his whole life and this one to his sister, for an insignificant price. But this didn't stop him to paint more than 800 paintings in his career;

• In 1954, Jimmy Denny, manager of Grand Ole Opry, fired Elvis Presley after only one concert. He told him: "You'll get nowhere, son. You'd better get back to driving trucks." Then Elvis made hit after hit, becoming one of the greatest singers of the world;

• Composer Ludwig van Beethoven was considered by his teachers "with no chance as a composer." He didn't listen to them and thus made five of his best symphonies being... completely deaf!

• Inventor Albert Einstein didn't speak until he was four and didn't read until he was seven. One of his teachers described him as being "a little slow, unsociable and lost forever in foolish dreams." He was expelled from school and lost admission at the Polytechnic University in Zurich. However, he learned to speak, read and even learn "some" math!

• An expert said about Vince Lombardi, who later became a great football player, that: "He possesses minimum knowledge about football and has total lack of motivation";

• Sportmen Michael Jordan and Bob Cousy were expelled from the high school basketball team. Jordan was saying: "I have failed many times in life. That's why I succeded!"

• Winston Churchill had to repeat the sixth grade as a student then every time he candidated he was defeated, until he was 62 years old and became Prime Minister. He later wrote: "Never should you recognize yourself as defeated, unless it's a thing of honour or good sense. Never, ever, should you give up!"

• In 1944, Emmeline Snively, the manager of a moddeling agency, told aspiring model Norma Jean Baker, "You'd better learn to be a secretary or to find a husband." Norma Jean became Marilyn Monroe, but no one has ever heard of Emmeline Snively!

• Charles Darwin gave up a career in medicine and his father told him: "You don't care about anything except catching dogs and rats." In his biography, Darwin wrote: "I was considered by my father and by all teachers as a very ordinary boy, actually lower than the average standard of intelligence";

• Sigmund Freud was booed on stage when he first presented his ideas to the scientific community in Europe. He got back to the office and continued his writing!

• Walt Disney was fired by a newspaper editor, being accused that he has no imagination or good ideas. He went bankrupt several times before he built Disneyland.

In fact, the idea proposed for the park was rejected on the grounds that it wouldn't attract anyone;

• Thomas Edison's teachers called him "too stupid to learn anything." He was fired from his first two jobs, being considered unproductive. As an inventor, he made over a thousand unsuccessful inventions before he was able to invent the light. Asked by a reporter how he felt failing over a thousand times, Edison said: "I didn't fail a thousand times, the light was an invention with a thousand steps."

• Charlie Chaplin was initially rejected by the studios in Hollywood, his pantonima being considered nonsense;

• At age 21, French actress Jeanne Moureau was told by a casting director that her head is too curved, that she's not pretty enough and isn't photogenic enough to make a movie. She took a deep breath and said: "All right then, I think I should do it my way." Having made a hundred movies, in 1997 she received the European Film Academy Award for Achievements throughout the career;

• When Pablo Casals reached 95 years old, a reporter asked him: "Mr. Casals, you are 95 years old and you're one of the greatest violoncellists of all time. Why are you still practicing six hours a day?" Casals answered, "Because I still think that I am making progress";

• Enrico Caruso's teacher told him that he has no voice

and can't sing at all. His parents would have wanted him to become an engineer. Eventually, Caruso was one of the most famous tenors in opera history, being one of the first 20 most famous artists of the twentieth century!

• Although it seems hard to believe Daniel Craig, the famous agent 007 James Bond was, before becoming an actor, homeless. He left his hometown and went to London for an acting career. But until he got a job, he was forced to sleep on a bench in a London park, having no money to afford renting a room;

• In 1970, the famous hero of action films, Sylvester Stallone lived for three weeks in a bus station in New York. But the star from Rambo escaped the ordeal, after having cought a role in a film where he made his debut as an actor. Thus he received for two days of filming the sum of two hundred dollars, with which he was able to rent a room to live decently.

And the examples can go on...

Source: http://oereneu785.wordpress.com/2011/10/14/
chestii-despre-perseverenta/
Source: http://www.apropo.ro/life-style/nu-te-da-niciodata-batut-vezi-17-exemple-de-
ambitie-si-perseverenta-6222831
http://www.libertatea.ro/detalii/articol/celebritati-saraci-Hollywood-
389128.html

We hear everywhere around us the urge "think positive". Often we perceive these words only as a welcome expression in times of sadness or crisis, but most often we don't leave room for any continuity in the depths of our consciousness. And this is not well at all ... let's look a little what kind of resonance our thoughts are sending into the universe, because the law of universal attraction is and will be valid regardless the type of energy to which we refer. It is already known and assumed by almost everyone that similar things attract each other, so if the signal sent by us will be positive, its echo will be similar, and if the signal sent by us will be full of negativity, envy, or other feeling of low resonance, we can't expect what we get back to register in another note. Of course, in order to distinguish that first we have to realize it and then use this information as a key to success.

Going forward based on the principles which are related to the law of attraction here are what could be the main coordinates of a positive attitude that might bring all the best in our life:

• First, if we want to change anything in your life we must first change the frequency of our thoughts;

• Our current thoughts decisively influence our future actions;

• To get the change we want in our lives, we must create the right energy and realize that through persistent thoughts;

• Memories that make us happy, friends, hobbies, music, prayer or anything we feel that we love are vital handy levers to change the frequency of the bad feelings with the one of good, positive things. Every man should create such tools for himself and to turn to them with confidence whenever he is sad and hopeless;

• It is known that the feeling of love has the highest frequency that we humans can emit and the more intense it will be, the greater the power that we can use;

• When sending thoughts and desires to the Universe is actually the moment when we clear up ourselves about what we really want, and when the heart and the mind converge towards the same goal, achieving it becomes only a matter of time and perseverance;

• If we draw in mind how we want the next day to look for us, we are able to better organize ourselves and we'll send to the universe the necessary details for our small and large challenges of that day to pass succesfully;

• You must use as little as possible the word "NO" and replace it with a milder formula, more conciliatory, which leaves room for positioning things in accordance with the universal harmony;

• When you have acquired the skills to use this wonderful gift which is being able to think positive, you'll have to use it in all aspects of life: career, human relationships and with your life partner, health, in fact in all that is related to everyday life. The quicker we understand and apply these truths, the more we'll have a longer life and beautifully lived that would fulfill and develop us in order to find our mission in our passage through this world.

P.S. However, success does not come as you say "I can ..." Positive thinking doesn't mean that you'll automatically achieve your dreams. Many believe that only this is enough ... You can't expect though that once you began thinking that you can get more money, the next day to find a suitcase full of money at your door. Success requires commitment, hard work and patience. Positive thinking will not automatically lead to the disappearance of all problems, but it means that if you believe in yourself, you act and you are persistent, you will achieve your dreams!

Source: Michael J. Losier, Law of attraction, M.M.S Publishing House, 2010
http://despresucces.ro/2012/12/30/gandirea-pozitiva-un-stil-de-viata/

THE END

THE END

"If you can profit from one thing shared to you by others, in return you are responsible itat your turn to share with others" - Chinese proverb

GOOD LUCK!!!

REFERENCES

REFERENCES:

Allan Pease, Body Language, Polimark Publishing House, Bucharest, 1993

Allan Pease, Body Language. How to read others' thoughts by their gestures, Polimark Publishing House, 1997

Allan&Barbara Pease, Communication Skills, Curtea Veche Publishing House, 2007

Ben Nogradi, When will you become a millionaire, Digital Data Publishing House, Cluj, 2005

Bogdan Ficeac, Manipulation Techniques (Second Edition), Nemira Publishing House, 1997

Burke Hedges, Dream-Biz.com, Curtea Veche Publishing House, 2003

Collet Peter, The Book of Tells. How can we read peoples' thoughts from their actions, Trei Publishing House, Bucharest, 2003

Cucos C., Psychopedagogy, Polirom Publishing House, 1998

Dinu M., Communication, Algos Publishing House, 2000

Source: *Don Failla, 45 Second Presentation That Will Change Your Life, Digital Data Publishing House, Cluj, 2004

Jeff Keller, Attitude is everything, Curtea Veche Publishing House, 2005

Leroy G., Dialogue in education, Polirom Publishing House, 1998

Michael J. Losier, Law of attraction, M.M.S Publishing House, 2010

Paun E., School Sociopedagogy, Educational & Pedagogic Publishing House, 1982

Richard Poe, The third wave, The new era in Network Marketing, Amaltea Publishing House, 1999

Richard Poe, The fourth wave, Network Marketing in the 21st Century, Amaltea Publishing House, 2002

Soitu L., Communication pedagogy, Educational & Pedagogic Publishing House, 1995

Stephen R. Covey, Seven Habits of Highly Effective People or Wisdom Alphabet, All Publishing House, 2009

Tom Hopkins, How to master the art of selling, Business Tech International Press, 2005

http://www.ziaronline.eu/2011/06/06/limbajul-nonverbal-in-negociere/

http://www.libertatea.ro/detalii/articol/celebritati-saraci-Hollywood-389128.html

www.ingramcontent.com/pod-product-compliance
Lightning Source LLC
Chambersburg PA
CBHW070437180526
45158CB00019B/1472